Affirmations
For The Inner Child

Rokelle Lerner

Health Communications, Inc.
Deerfield Beach, Florida

Publisher: Health Communications, Inc.
         3201 S.W. 15th Street
         Deerfield Beach, Florida 33442-8124

Cover design by Reta Thomas
Illustration: Barbara Nolf-Wood

Dedication

To my daughters Mer and Sasha whose lives have been an inspiration and a continual affirmation of humanity blessed by Divinity.

Acknowledgments

The author wishes to acknowledge the contributions of the following individuals:

>Naomi Lucks
>Patrick Means
>Laura Littleford
>Mer Lerner
>Lissa Halls-Johnson
>Joann Ricketts
>Lois Weisberg

Editor: Kathleen Michels

Introduction

All of us need positive affirmation throughout our lives. As children, these powerful messages helped us to know that we were worthwhile, that it was all right to want food, to be touched and that our very existence was a precious gift. The messages that we received from our parents helped us to form decisions that determined the course of our lives.

If we were raised with consistent, nurturing parents, we conclude that life is meaningful and that people are to be trusted. If we were raised with parents who were addictively or compulsively ill, we determine that life is threatening and chaotic — that we are not deserving of joy. These are the crucial decisions that impact our lives long after we have forgotten them.

Unfortunately, childhood judgments don't disappear. They remain as dynamic forces that contaminate our adulthood. When childhood needs are not taken care of because of abuse or abandonment, we spend our lives viewing the world through the distorted perception of a needy infant or an angry adolescent. The more we push these child parts away, the more control they have over us. This denial of our inner child manifests in destructive ways: dependent relationships, sabotaged successes, somatic illnesses and dysfunctional parenting.

In order to end this cycle of suffering, we must embrace our inner child at whatever age and stage it shows itself to us. The daily readings in this book address the screaming infant, the precocious toddler and the feisty two-year-old who still waits for the parent who will make them feel safe, loved and accepted. Through the use of this book, we learn the skill of reparenting. At last, we can become the loving parents to our internal children and take charge of our lives.

Affirmations For The Inner Child is dedicated to those adults who are ready to heal their childhood wounds. It is through this courageous effort that we will move from a life of pain into recovery.

Rokelle Lerner

This year I will create positive memories.

Today is the dawn of a new year. It is the day when many people reflect on the past and how they will change in the coming year. For many, it is a day of hope and new beginnings. For me, it has often been a day of terror as I face all the days that stretch out before me. Will I fail? Will I fall back into old destructive patterns of behavior?

This day often reminds me of the alcoholism I would rather forget. Memories of childhood disappointments, arguments and violence mar the festivities of this day.

This day I will look back only to rejoice in what I have accomplished in the year past. I will concentrate only on today. I will make the best decisions I can for this day alone, not trying to tackle my whole future. This year I will create positive memories to replace the old.

Today I listen to the needs of my infant.

I am a newborn baby. After nine months within your womb, it will take some time for me to be fully here. Being born was difficult; all I want to do right now is to sleep curled up in a ball.

Slowly day by day, I open up. One finger stretches out, then another. Soon my hand is open to receive yours. One leg kicks, and then another. Soon I am waving my feet in the air, enjoying my energy. One arm reaches out, then the other and I am able to return your hug. My eyes open and focus on your loving face. I smile at the sound of your voice. I feel myself fully in the world, ready for adventure.

As I confront new issues and repair old childhood wounds, infancy themes will arise for me. Instead of feeling shameful, I will seek out those I trust for holding, touching and nurturing. I am learning to be the loving parent to the precious infant inside of me.

My precious inner child is not afraid.

When I was a child, I was terrified of the dark. There were monsters under the bed and in the closet. Burglars might break in at any moment. Night sounds were a cause for alarm, shadows were menacing. So I learned to shut my eyes and go to sleep until morning, when the terror would be gone.

Now I know that dark holds no terror but my own fear. Tonight I will make friends with the darkness. I will listen for the night sounds and discover what they really are. That slowly opening door is a tree creaking. I hear the sound of people on night shifts driving their cars to work. I hear babies crying to be held.

As I listen with my new night ears and see with my new night vision, I discover that life continues in the dark as surely as it does in the light and that both together make one whole day.

On this day I begin a new life.

New Year's Day has come and gone and I am relieved. By the time I was 10 years old, I knew that the start of the new year with all its joy and celebration was a hoax. It wasn't the threshold to a new beginning. Promises would be broken and dreams shattered just as they had been the year before and the year before that. So what's the big deal?

Today I will hug my inner child and make this solemn promise:

I will not carry the heavy baggage of hurt and disappointment with me into this new year. I will forgive myself for the pain I have caused myself and others. I will forgive others for having caused me pain. On this day of new beginnings, I will begin a new life.

I will allow my inner child
to receive constructive criticism.

Inside of me lives a 12-year-old who takes every remark as a criticism. This child transforms every comment into a judgment of her self-worth: "You're bad. You can't do anything right." So she plants her feet, puts her hands on her hips, and yells back: "Shut up! You can't tell me what to do!" I'm worn out by her angry, combative stance.

Today I will allow my inner child to receive constructive criticism. I can listen to the feedback from others without becoming defensive. I can take some time to reflect on it and ask myself, "Does this behavior need to change?" I no longer have the need to say, "You are wrong" to make myself "right." My inner self is already right. I can change my actions to reflect her shining image.

My adolescent within is learning order.

As a teenager, I hated it when my mom told me to clean my room. It was my room, wasn't it? I could decide how I wanted to live. So, in rebellion, I made certain my bedroom was always a mess — shoes and clothes and worse strewn on the floor.

As an adult, I'm still stuck with my rebellious teenager. Sometimes I think his piles of trash will bury me. Cleaning up after him leaves me angry and exhausted.

Today I will take control of my environment. I no longer have to feel overwhelmed by the enormity of housekeeping tasks. I make my own messes and I will clean them up. When I have finished using something, I will put it back. I make sure I am not inadvertently bringing the outside inside. I will work with, instead of against myself. Today my environment will reflect my inner accord.

Today I will sing a joyful song
with my inner child.

Young children love to sing. They do not study voice in Italy before they sing an operetta about the events of their day. They do not wait to sell a million records before they croon a lullaby. Singing to them is another way of speaking.

My inner child loves to sing along with the radio. I may feel self-conscious but Pavarotti and Aretha Franklin really don't mind if my voice drowns them out. In the business of the day, I forget that I can sing and wash the dishes at the same time — but my inner child knows I can.

Everyone is given the gift of song. I do not have to have perfect pitch to claim it. I do not have to perform for others to enjoy it. Today I will sing along with my inner child and together we will make a joyful song.

I can set my own boundaries.

No! No, I won't! No, thank you. Simple words, yet difficult to say. A two-year-old says no to test the limits of others, to see where the lines are drawn.

In a dysfunctional home there are no boundaries, no limits. There is little or no supervision to make certain a child is safe in his attempts to learn about the world. As a child I learned the world is dangerous and uncertain, not safe.

Today I will say no when my boundaries are invaded. I will say no if someone wants me to do something that goes against my beliefs, feelings or desires. It's okay to say no when I'm tired. It's okay to say no to something I don't like. It's okay to set my own boundaries.

I can make a mess and enjoy it.

In my childhood home, cleanliness was next to godliness and making a mess was bad. I was not allowed to play in the dirt, make mud pies, paint my body instead of the paper, wipe my dirty fingers on my clothes. And God forbid that I should track dirt into the house! I quickly learned how to be good: Keep clean. Don't make a mess.

My inner child needs to experience the wonder of feeling soft wet glops of earth in her hands, the delight of watching mud snakes coil out from between her toes. She needs to know that she is of the earth.

Today I will allow the two-year-old within me the joy of getting dirty and messy. I may put on some old, comfortable clothes and go for a romp in the woods. Or I may get down on my hands and knees in my garden. I love the cool soil on my skin, the sharp, tangy smell. No matter what I choose to do, I will feel a part of the earth.

**I radiate inner light in this
season of darkness.**

New life is conceived and nurtured in restful darkness. Seeds planted below the ground protect the young plant from cold and wind. The seed lies dormant and waits for the right season to begin its growth.

As an adult child, I sometimes feel impatient with my progress. "Day by day" sounds hollow to my ears when I feel I'm stuck on a plateau.

I will remember that each plateau is a place to gather my energy for the next change. I will treat myself with patience and gentleness during this time of unseen growth.

Today I will welcome the stages of my inner child's development. In this season of lengthening nights, I radiate the inner light of new life.

I can meet my own needs.

Today I will take responsibility for meeting my own needs. I will break free of the destructive bonds of dependency forged by my dysfunctional family.

Because of the smothering, controlling love that I received as a child, I became passively dependent on others to meet my needs. Not allowed to tell others what I wanted, I expected them to discern my needs automatically by reading my mind. As a result, I was always angry because I was constantly being let down by others who were failing to "make" me happy.

Today I will help my inner child take a giant step toward growing up. I will begin to tell others what I need, instead of hoping that they will guess. Whether or not they are able to give me what I need, I will take responsibility for my own happiness. I will do those things that bring me the greatest satisfaction. And I will live this day with a joy and a contentment that come from myself, not from those around me.

I celebrate my passage.

I celebrate my passage from childhood to adult. It was quite a struggle but I made it through those stormy seas of uncertainty in one piece!

As a child, growing up was not something I wanted to do. All I had to do was take a good look at the adults in my life. They always seemed tired, unhappy and hassled. If that was what was in store for me, I wanted no part of it.

I know today that maturity doesn't mean the death of my inner child. Maturity means that I can gain insight from my experiences. Maturity means that I can balance the spontaneous and the rational, my child within with my adult wisdom.

Today I celebrate my adulthood.

The child within me is sexually alive.

With my recovery has come a wonderful new freedom to enjoy my sexuality. Today I will celebrate my sexuality in appropriate ways without fear and without shame.

The child within me has taken years to heal from the shaming and abuse inflicted during her childhood. She was taught to think of herself as a bad person and of her body as evil. Instead of a wonderful God-given gift, sex was considered dirty, something to be ashamed of. As I have loved my little one toward health and wholeness, many of these old internal messages have faded into silence. Feeling good about who I am as a person has made me feel good about my sexuality. I see now that how I feel about my physical self is a mirror of how I feel about my core self. Today I will enjoy who I am as a sexual being, for sexuality is one of God's marvelous gifts to me.

I am resourceful in helping my inner child.

Children enjoy both receiving and giving help. A young child will ask anyone — a parent, a stranger, the governor of the state — to help them fasten a difficult zipper or buckle. A young child will also eagerly offer to help a parent wash the dishes.

While growing up, I received mixed messages from my parents, "You can ask for help but don't disturb me." I felt shame for having need and I learned that there were strings attached for any assistance given to me. As a result, I learned to silence my requests for help.

Today I welcome the requests of my inner child. I respond with attentiveness and resourcefulness. I am able to ask for help when I need it and I respond to others' needs out of free choice rather than guilt. As my ability to give and receive becomes healthier, I am able to attend to my inner child.

I rejoice in my aliveness.

As a child, I was afraid my mother and my father would die and I would be left an orphan. Terrified, I hung on for dear life. For years I lived in fear of my own death. I constantly questioned: What if I should die? Will it be painful? How will it happen? When will it happen? Today? A year from now? I grew to fear anything that I thought might cause my death. I cut my risks — and my opportunities — to the bare minimum.

In my effort not to die, I had no life.

At this moment I am alive. My acceptance of my own mortality sets me free to live my life. My life is a shining jewel bound by the finite limits of birth and death. All that I can know and feel is right here, right now. This moment is all there is, and at this moment I am alive.

Today I will rejoice in my aliveness and live every moment to the fullest.

I will move ahead when things go wrong.

One of the major challenges of my recovery has been overcoming the negative programming from my childhood. Chaos and catastrophe were all I knew in my dysfunctional family, so I grew up expecting life to turn out badly. A large part of my inner work has been to discard my expectations of catastrophe and replace them with positive expectations.

Yet the hammer blows of life still threaten to break apart the recovery scaffolding I've so carefully erected. When I'm disappointed or feeling lonely, the old tapes begin to play inside my head. "You'll never find happiness," they mock.

Today when reversals happen in my life, I will not take them as evidence of certain doom. Instead I will reaffirm my belief in my own success. I will review how far I have come in my journey toward health and wholeness. Today I will move ahead with optimism and with faith in myself.

I reward my inner child for good behavior.

As a child, I was punished for being bad, obstinate, stupid, wrong, forgetful, lazy — you name it, I was punished whether I deserved it or not. I never seemed to get any better. I just became an expert at blaming myself for all my misdeeds.

My inner child is starved for praise. I no longer will beat him up for his failings. Instead I will praise him for behaving in ways that support his growth. I'll make sure he understands that some of his *actions* are incorrect, not his soul. As I speak to my inner child, I will use a gentle tone filled with love and admiration.

I am proud of my ability to take positive, constructive action as I learn to reparent myself. I know that the essence of who I am is always good. That never changes!

I affirm the wisdom of my inner voice.

Today I affirm the wisdom of my inner voice and the richness of the basic intelligence my Higher Power has given me. When I listen to my inner voice and exercise my intelligence, I make very good decisions.

As a child, I was taught not to think for myself, not to trust or value my own inner voice. My parents fostered dependence and I discounted my own wisdom. I came to rely exclusively on others' input for my decisions.

As I grew into adulthood, I silenced my intuition altogether and, as a result, made many poor decisions that caused me pain. I have since learned from my mistakes and have at last come to trust the wisdom of my inner voice. It is a powerful ally on my journey through life, prompting me to make sustaining and nurturing decisions and helping me to avoid destructive ones.

Today I will affirm the wisdom of my inner voice and honor my ability to make good decisions.

I can learn from other people.

As a child, I had no heroes. I didn't want to emulate any of the adults in my life. I set out to make my own way and my own rules in life.

Now I think I've gone about as far as I can on my own. As an adult, I can see the need for someone after whom I can model my behavior. I need to find a person, who exemplifies what I want to be "when I grow up." I need to find a good guide and teacher who can be patient with my slips and supportive of my efforts because she or he has already been down this road.

Today I will start my search for a therapist, sponsor or coach whom I admire and trust. I no longer have to "go it alone." There are people in my life from whom I can learn — people who would be glad, even honored, to help me.

I reach out to touch everything.

When I was a toddler, I reached out to touch everything — the soft fur coats of enormous women, my mother's hot iron, the pebbly dirt in the driveway, the glistening pots and pans in the cupboards, the bright knickknacks in a neighbor's house. My curiosity was not okay, for I was constantly reproached, "Get your hands off that! Keep your hands to yourself!" Soon I learned to look but not touch. I learned my lesson well. Now as an adult, I keep the world at an arm's distance. I observe rather than engage in life. My reticence about reaching out has kept me disconnected from myself, my environment and other people.

Today I will give free rein to the curious toddler within me. I will explore the textures of the world: smooth, rough, pebbly, gritty, wet, dry, hot, cold, sticky, sooty, cool, warm. I will reach out to touch the world around me.

I am lovable at every age.

As a child, I was at once fascinated and repelled by old people. Their wrinkly rough faces were so different from my smooth glowing cheeks. They smelled like sour milk or heavy perfume. An old smell. They couldn't move as quickly as I could. They ran out of energy. They hated noise. Their future held only sickness and death. I swore I would never grow old.

At this unique moment in my adult life, I take the opportunity to look at both the past and the future with clear vision. As I look back at my child self, I respect the feelings I had then. Yet I see them for what they are: the perceptions of a child made through the distorted lens of childhood. As I look forward to my aged self, I respect the self I will become, the self who unashamedly wears the scars and signs of having lived a full life.

At this moment I love and respect all of what I was, am and will be. We are joined forever in a warm, loving embrace.

I will welcome my dreams as teachers.

My childhood nightmares were so scary that I never wanted to remember them. Often I was afraid to go to bed. I only wanted to sleep peacefully and not dream.

As an adult, I understand that I can learn from my dreams. If I pay attention to them, they will tell me things I am too busy to learn during the day. My dreams can be humorous, expressing themselves in puns. I can learn to laugh in my dreams, I can teach myself to fly, I can communicate with lost friends and relatives. I can speak with deeper levels of myself.

Of course, I can have bad dreams, too. When I do, I will surround myself and my inner child with warmth and reassuring words: "Nothing can hurt you. I will take care of you now." I have the power to disarm any nightmare. I no longer have to be overwhelmed by terror.

Today I will be playful.

Today I will let myself be playful without worrying about whether it fits my image as a responsible adult.

As a child in my addicted family, I was forced to hurry and grow up. I took on adult responsibilities, such as substitute spouse and/or substitute parent. As a result, I developed a serious approach to life at the expense of my sense of playfulness. As I have matured, I have come to realize that there's more to life than seriousness and responsibility. Real health for me also includes playfulness, lightheartedness and spontaneity.

Today I will give my inner child the freedom to play. I will give rein to my spontaneous impulses without worrying about being perfectly responsible. I will take a more playful approach to my work, too.

Already I feel release of the tension that comes from being overly responsible as I resolve to live more playfully today.

I am willing to receive love.

I am willing to receive love.

Love is the food my infant self needs to survive and the universe exists to provide that love. Like a baby, I open my mouth and take love in. I feel the sweet honey of love pour into my body, filling me with warm comfort. I hear love in all the sounds of life: the birds chattering in the trees, the wind blowing between the buildings, the laughter of children playing. I feel love in the touch of others, in the tongue of a dog licking my face, in the sun's rays. I open my eyes and see love in the faces of everyone I meet. I am filled to overflowing.

Love is available to me in many forms. Today I will broaden my rigid notions of how love is to be packaged and delivered. I will open myself to receiving the vast expressions of God's love in this world.

Today is exactly as it should be.

Sometimes I feel tyrannized by my critical inner voices. "Dumb!" they rage, "Stupid! Incompetent!" They are merciless when I make even the smallest mistake, slicing away at my self-esteem.

Today I will be gentle with myself. I will contemplate the meaning of what it means to heal. Healing means that today is exactly as it should be. It means that I already possess everything I need to be a sane, healthy, whole human being.

Now I have a decision to make. Either I can become obsessed about my blemishes which will open me to the attacks of my critical inner voices. Or I can back off and take a more expansive view of myself. Today I choose to take the life-giving view of who I am. I know I am exactly where I should be at this point of my journey.

I can see clearly now.

Today I will use my mind to discern between fantasy and reality.

As a child, I often retreated into fantasy to block out the pain of living in a dysfunctional family. Whenever the conflict and chaos around me was too great, I withdrew into my idealized world. In my adult life, this habit of mental retreat hinders me from dealing with my world as it really is.

Today I will analyze the difference between fantasy and reality in my personal and my professional life. This means I will take time to step out of the fog and look clearly at myself and my relationships. I no longer need to withdraw into my fantasy world when life becomes too scary, for I am a competent person able to meet every challenge. I can create a real life for myself and my inner child, a life that satisfies and delights.

I can let go of the need to be self-critical.

Today I will let go of the need to be self-critical.

It has always been important to me to be the first to criticize myself. I think that if I get there before someone else does, I can spare myself the pain of being found lacking. In doing so, however, I inflict constant pain on myself and, what is worse, create a false self-image that tricks others into seeing me in the same unflattering way.

Today I will stop looking at myself through the distorting dark glasses of self-criticism. Instead of focusing only on my defects, I will look at myself in the light and accept myself for the wonderfully complex being that I am. And just maybe, this is how others will see me, too.

**Today I will contemplate the
source of my strength.**

The house is quiet. My heart is not. My children
lie sleeping on this hot afternoon. The blinds
gently slap the windows.

Evidence of my successes hangs on the wall
before me. Symbols of the love of friends lie
here and there on my desk. Encouraging words
are placed about where I can easily see them.
Yet past successes, the love of friends and encouraging words don't seem to help me break
through the uneasiness, dissatisfaction and fear.

So I will take time out to talk to my Higher
Power. I need to hand over, one by one, the
things that are disturbing my peace. I give
them in exchange for a new peace that can
come only from meditating on the source of
my strength.

I allow others into my life.

As a child, I was hugged too tight, smothered in the embraces of grown-ups I didn't like. I wanted to push them away but I wasn't allowed to — they were the adults and they could do whatever they liked. So I learned to shut them out with my mind. I curled into a tight ball deep inside, the only position in which I felt safe.

I do not want to live like this anymore. It's lonely in here. I'm sick of living in constant tension with the world. I'm ready to come out.

Today I will allow my inner child to relax and welcome others into her world. I know there is enough room here for people who treat me with respect and kindness. I can protect myself and still allow others into my life.

I am allowing myself to love.

"Love hurts," the song goes. So many times I have given love that has not been returned. As a child, I was the one who loved my parents unconditionally. Wasn't it supposed to be the other way around? Many painful years later I realized that my parents were unable to love me in a healthy way. As I grew up, I chose people to love who weren't capable of loving me. My relationships have left me depleted, hurt and hopeless. And somewhere deep inside I made a decision to stop loving.

Today I will allow myself to love again. I will love without fear of being depleted, for I will use the wisdom of my experience to guide me. I will start slowly, experimenting with different ways of loving. I will greet a stranger with my smile or the sparkle of my eyes. I will love my family and friends with the touch of my hand, words of kindness and support. My love is healing and I learn to share it with others.

I celebrate my passage into adolescence.

My passage into adolescence went unmarked. No longer a child, not yet an adult, I didn't know who I was or where I was going. I felt set adrift on a river to nowhere. Those years were marked by shame, confusion and wildly fluctuating moods, emotions and hormones. The residue of those unresolved years is still with me.

Today I will celebrate my passage from childhood into adolescence. It is the end of one life stage, the beginning of another. Now I can acknowledge my anxiety, pain, confusion, heartache, passion and even rebellion. I can face the unanswered questions about the meaning of life, sex or death. I can acknowledge this time for its positive aspects: the chaotic profusion of new growth, the wild energy of life seeking expression. I celebrate my adolescence as a time of great change, great peril, great power. I feel strong in my ability to navigate through these turbulent waters to the calm bay of adulthood.

Today I notice the wonders of the world.

How do the stars stay up in the sky? Where does the white go when the snow melts? Where does the wind come from? In the process of becoming a grown-up, what happened to my sense of awe and wonder? It is hard to praise the creation of the world when you are involved with survival. In my rush to grow up, I missed out on some very soul-enriching experiences.

I know that the child within me is still very much alive and anxious to awaken some of my sleeping parts. The excitement and adventure for life is still available if I choose attitudes that make it so.

As I free myself from the constricting blinders of my dysfunctional family, I am able to enjoy the wonderment of the world around me.

Today I will be open to delightful surprises.

Today I will reclaim my joy in surprises. Life holds many delightful surprises in unexpected places and at unexpected times.

When I was growing up, surprises always seemed to bring pain and disappointment, not joy. I learned early to see life in muted colors; I didn't expect much of anything. Each day was like the day before. The dull sameness felt safe.

Today I will let joyous surprises into my life and watch the face of my inner child shine. I will thrill to the fact that I do not know exactly what will happen to me today. I may have a quiet surprise. I may look down at a crack in the gray pavement and see a tiny flower growing there despite all odds. I may have a pleasant surprise. I may look up with a smile and have a stranger return my smile. I will surprise myself with my reclaimed ability to feel wonder.

I am learning to say goodbye.

When I first learned my friend would be leaving, I was wild with grief. I felt like a child afraid of being abandoned, terrified of being alone.

I hold my inner child and explain, "Sometimes you have to learn to say goodbye to a friend whose path differs from yours. It's hard to let go and it's scary. But when a friendship isn't growing any more, you have to let it go."

Today my friend and I have come to a fork in the road. My friend must take one path and I must take the other. I am saddened by the parting but I rejoice in our ability to go our separate ways to fulfill our own needs. Our parting need not be forever. Perhaps, farther down the road, our paths will cross again.

Today I will listen to my inner wisdom.

Sometimes I listen too much to the harsh, commanding voices that buzz inside my head: "Don't disobey your teacher. Father knows best. Do what adults tell you to do. Behave yourself. Act your age. If you're lost, ask a police officer for help." I am a child who listens to authority and obeys without thinking. But those old voices do not always have my best interests at heart.

Today I will still those chattering voices. I will muffle noise until it fades away altogether. I want to hear only one voice, the strong, clear voice of my own inner wisdom. Deep within is a strong, knowing self whose wisdom astounds me. Today I will listen as words of wise counsel resonate throughout my whole being.

I do know what is right for me. I carry my own answers within me. If I listen, I will hear.

I celebrate my inner child.

No one made much of me when I was growing up. My parents sleepwalked through birthdays and holidays. I got what *they* wanted me to have. They never gave me gifts I really wanted or needed because they were too preoccupied with their own problems. To them I was a duty, not a passion. I need to make up for all the celebrations my inner child missed.

I celebrate my inner child in many ways. Sometimes I buy her gifts — a bouquet of flowers, a book or a special present she's longed for over the years. Sometimes I surprise her with a weekend away, a massage or a special meal. Sometimes we go to the zoo or see a movie on the spur of the moment.

I look for opportunities to celebrate my inner child's achievements. Most of the time I celebrate her — just because she's her.

I am an actor — not a reactor.

Today I will talk about my angry feelings rather than just blowing up. My uncontrolled outbursts damage those I love and shatter all possible lines of clear communication.

My parents provided no positive model of how to deal with emotions in a healthy way. Anger was either repressed entirely or spewed forth in rage or cutting criticism. I learned to stuff my anger, only to have it suddenly explode like a volcano. I no longer want to be controlled by my parents' example or by the reactions of the child within me. He is emotionally stuck between being a "terrible" two-year-old and a rebellious adolescent. I will not allow him to control my life any longer.

Today if I feel hurt or angry, I will talk about my feelings instead of just blowing up. I am responsible for my own happiness and peace of mind.

Today I celebrate the inner girl or inner boy as an exciting surprise gift.

Today I welcome my inner child as the girl or boy I was created to be. My gender was given to me by my Higher Power, and I accept my gift with gratitude and joy.

While I was growing up, my parents conveyed spoken and unspoken messages that I was born the wrong sex. They had their minds set on a certain number of boys and girls, in a certain order: first a son, then a daughter, then another son. With my birth, their plans came to naught. On various occasions, I felt I was "wrong" from the very beginning. They rarely failed to remind me of how I had shattered their expectations. Today I acknowledge that I am a human, not a number or a factor in someone else's plan. I am not responsible for meeting another's needs or expectations. The gift of my gender belongs to me and I began as an exciting surprise.

I enjoy my successes.

My parents did not know how to praise me; they only knew how to discourage me. The only successes I ever got credit for were the ones that reflected well on them, not the ones that had meaning for me. I soon learned that it was pointless to share my enthusiasms and small achievements with them. Finally, I stopped thinking of anything I did as important. As an adult, I often don't recognize my achievements unless someone else points them out to me, and then I don't know how to react. I hold back my smile and push away my enthusiasm until it disappears.

Today I will praise my inner child for her achievements, knowing that even the smallest deserves recognition. I am proud of her ideas and her efforts. Her voice grows stronger, her eyes shine with pride in herself as each day she tells me of her progress. Empowered by this feeling, she understands that she is worthy of success.

I love from my strength and my power.

I love from my inner strength and my personal power. My power creates healthy love, which manifests itself through caring, knowledge, responsibility and respect. My love is a reflection of my free choice and my ability to respond powerfully.

In our culture, love is romanticized as a mystifying, random whirl of passion that *happens* to a person. Falling in love is thought to be the culmination of love. Yet, love is only meaningful and lasting when a person chooses to love responsibly and welcomes the opportunity to allow love to grow and deepen with time.

Today I will love myself by genuinely caring for my own well-being. I will choose to love those people who deserve my love and respect its strength and power.

Today I am learning to surrender.

I have a frightened four-year-old inside who fears that relinquishing control means the world will fall apart. It was difficult to "let go" in a home where spontaneity brought criticism and violence.

As an adult, I realize that my attempts to control have resulted in incessant struggle and frustration. Today I will consider what it would be like if I gradually give up my hypervigilant effort to dominate life.

If I relinquish control of most things in my life, my world will not fall apart. A river has powerful currents that pull and tug. A leaf in the river survives by going with the flow, not trying to control it. I can be safe and happy without trying to maintain rigid control over the world around me.

Today I discover the path of discovery and joy.

I feel a strong desire to reach out and explore today — to go places I've never gone, do things I've never done. I sense bottled-up feelings I've never felt before, feelings waiting to be elicited by new experiences, new discoveries.

Yet the toddler within hesitates . . . "The world's too dangerous for you!" This message came from parents who, driven by their own addictive needs and insecurities, wanted only to control. And so I've played out my life within the narrow circle of the familiar. But as I've grown, this narrow circle has become confining, suffocating. There is so much in this world that I have yet to experience!

Today I will say no to the broken records of fear from the past. And I will say yes to the innocent curiosity of the toddler within me, yes to the path of growth and discovery and joy.

I am breaking free from negative patterns.

Becoming invisible kept me from great harm when I was a child. Hiding my true self helped me survive in my family. Invisibility became my refuge.

As an adult, becoming invisible doesn't help me anymore. When I am invisible to myself, I ignore my needs and deny my emotions. I don't want to risk showing others who I really am.

Today I give myself permission to come out of hiding. I no longer need to be invisible to feel safe. I choose to break free from that childhood pattern.

Because I am a vital human being, I will participate fully in life without fear of negative consequences. I can enjoy who I am and those around me will enjoy me as well.

**My personal power adds structure
for my inner child.**

My personal power and my needs are inseparable. As I widen my participation in the
world about me, I assert both my power and
my needs.

As a young child growing up in a dysfunctional
family, I could not express either my power or
my needs. I curbed my desires and limited my
scope of possibilities.

As I recover, my world is no longer limited to a
small canvas but a large mural. As my needs
become more varied, I paint not just with
primary colors but with all the hues in the
rainbow. My personal power adds structure,
focus and knowledge to my vision of what my
world can be.

In recovery, I present my inner child with an
exciting vision of the world that I observe and
shape. I dare to express passionate desires and
I commit my personal power to seeking my
own fulfillment.

I am open to giving and receiving love.

On this Valentine's Day, I celebrate my ability to love myself and others in a balanced relationship of give-and-take.

I let go of the heartaches of addictive relationships. I am no longer prey to being a victim "shot with the arrow of love." I no longer need to "fall in love." I can *be* in love, with my feet firmly planted on the ground and my arms around my lover. I can *grow* into love, with the emotions of an adult and the excitement of a child.

Today I rejoice in my ability to love myself unconditionally and with respect. In doing so, I have more of myself available to love others.

**Today I will stretch my imagination and
experience new powers of vision.**

What if my eyes were on my elbows? Then I
could see behind me when I walked. Would
that mean I would have to walk backward?

When children begin to reason, their powers of
imagination grow stronger. They allow their
creativity to produce a world where anything is
possible: What if walls could speak? What if
trees could walk?

By speaking and walking in new ways, children
broaden their own sense of personal power.
Dreaming great dreams becomes less fantastic
and more real. They know how to move like the
trees; they know how to tell tall stories. Today
I will listen when my inner child asks, "What
if . . . ?" Today I will stretch my imagination
and experience new powers of vision.

I accept my friends for who they are.

Today I will allow my friends to be themselves. If they make mistakes, that's okay, they're human just like me. If they hurt my feelings, we can talk it out.

Before I began to recover, I had a hard time keeping friends. The first time they did something I didn't like I felt betrayed and cut them off. I reasoned, "If they really knew me or cared about me, they wouldn't have disappointed me." My co-dependency left me with rigid standards that no one could live up to.

Now I allow my friends to be themselves — in all their imperfection — and they allow me to be me. We accept each other just as we are. Our mutual acceptance is the foundation of our friendship.

I have the courage to slow down.

I need to take time alone just to be still and to reflect on life. In the midst of the pain in my childhood home, taking time to think was the last thing I wanted to do. I sought to push away the hurtful realities of my family life by being involved in a whirl of activity.

Now as an adult, my frenetic activity chokes life out of my spirit. As I become mentally and physically exhausted, I know that my survival depends on learning to slow down. So today I will make a conscious effort. I will walk, not run. I will say no to friends and co-workers who want me to do just "one more thing."

As I decrease my hectic pace, I notice old feelings surface that need to be felt. I will give my attention to one emotion at a time, asking what it is there to tell me. I will have the courage to slow down and feel.

My inner child belongs to the winning team.

Today I choose the winning team on which my inner child belongs. The child within me is a winner and I will find the team that deserves me. In school, I felt excluded when classmates picked teams for a game. The captains stood in front of my class and chose the players one by one. I often was one of the last to be chosen. When my name was finally called, I felt ashamed.

Today I belong to the winning team of growth and recovery and I can belong to other winning teams, too. I may join a sports team where my participation is valued. If I want, I may take lessons and develop my athletic skills. Or I may find other teams — book clubs, painting classes, support groups — where my contributions will be acknowledged.

I can write my own story.

It seems as though I repeat the same old lines I learned as a child. I always seem to be involved in the same plot — I can predict the beginning, middle and outcome of my life situations. I sit back, passively observing my life as if it were a movie I've seen a hundred times before.

Well, this movie needs a new director and I'm hired! Today I will say, "Cut! Let's start over again with a new script. I'm in charge and I want new characters, new motivations, new set designs. I want to be surprised by the plot's twists and turns. I want to hear the lines read in fresh, exciting ways."

My life is *my* movie. My name will be in big letters as the star of the show. This movie will not be a grade B film that's cheap and boring. Rather, this film will be a work of art — an epic!

I will savor each moment today.

Chocolate ice cream, a child savors every drop. She eats her cone slowly, relishing each bit. Even when the ice cream drips all over her hand, she doesn't care, preferring to lick it off later. Concerned about dirty clothes and car, mother tries to rush the process. Yet nothing can rush this child.

I can take a lesson from this child, for I speed through life at such a pace that I hardly notice where I am, or how I feel. Many times I gulp my meals. I ride to work, arriving at my destination without noticing anything but the car in front of me. I rush through work, sex, relationships and parenting without being fully present.

Today I will practice savoring life. I will choose to share a meal with someone I enjoy and taste each bite. I will notice the texture of the chair in which I sit, the colorful place settings on the table. I will see my reflection shine in the sparkle of my companion's eyes.

I don't have to act cute to be loved.

I was a cute kid and I traded on it from day one. All I had to do was look coy or entertain people to get what I wanted. It was easy but it wasn't real. Deep inside, I always knew that I was fooling others and that I couldn't coast on my cute looks and charming ways forever. I knew that I wasn't learning how to do things for myself. Worse, I was deeply afraid that if others knew the real me, they wouldn't love me at all.

Today I will allow my cute child to be herself. Yes, she's cute but that's not all she is. I respect her ability to determine what she needs and to ask for it directly. I love her for being herself.

**Today I will use my memories
to mark my growth.**

Memorials of war, destroyed lives and victories punctuate the serene park in the middle of town. All are crafted of cement and bronze to survive the years so no one will ever forget.

Memorials stand within my memory. Memorials of my past wars, of my wounds and the devastated lives of family and friends. Words raised in bronze stand out to remind me of what took place, of the pain that will never completely go away.

It is my choice whether to use each memorial as a stone wall to inhibit my growth or as a marker of my growth. I can visit those markers to contemplate the past, knowing full well I do not have to live there. Today I will praise myself for how far I have come in my emotional healing.

I will make time in my life for play.

When older children play games, they follow the rules without adult supervision. As part of creative play, they may change a game by altering the rules or they may create a new game with new rules. In this way, children create rules that serve their needs; they learn that order is both secure and flexible.

In my family of origin, I had no time to play games with other children. My studies and my chores were deemed more important. On the rare occasions when I was allowed to play, I felt guilty. I did not learn to create rules that worked for me as a child or as an adult.

Today I will find a game that my inner child wants to play. I may invite a friend to play cards or checkers. We can play by the rules or we can create a new game with new rules. Today I will affirm my right to create rules that meet my needs. I will make time in my life for play.

I experiment with life one step at a time.

Sometimes my life feels as if I'm trying to cross a creek filled with rocks and cold rushing water. My feet try hard to avoid the cold as I focus on the rock ahead. I gauge the distance and jump. Balancing on that rock, I search for another stepping stone. When I find it, I carefully take the step. I repeat the pattern again and again until the other side of the creekbed becomes reality beneath my feet. In life, I cannot always know the end result. Sometimes I see only one step at a time. I'm not sure what that next step will bring. What if it's too slippery and I fall into the icy water? If I fall will someone laugh? Will I be hurt?

Thanks to my recovery, panic no longer consumes me when I can see only one step ahead. I can take that step, knowing the next will follow once I safely reach my foothold. And if I should fall, I know I will still reach the opposite shore a little wiser than if I hadn't fallen.

I can touch and be touched.

Today I will affirm myself as a sensual being. I will nurture my inner child and myself, by giving and receiving physical affection.

As a baby and later as a child, my needs to be touched, talked to and held with affection went unmet. A hunger born of neglect developed inside me, a yearning to be touched and lovingly held. Because my parents didn't touch me, I was certain that no one would ever want to touch me. As an adult, I resist my need to touch and be touched by becoming stiff and tense. I often act blase — or tough to keep my deepest fear a secret: the fear that I am unlovable.

Reaching out to others with spontaneous affection can release within me a wellspring of joy. Today I will reach out and celebrate my ability to touch and be touched.

Today I will do what is right for me.

As a child, I often changed what I wanted to do because others didn't want to do it. I changed what I felt because others told me not to feel it. This adaptability has carried over into my adult life. Yes, the ability to adapt is good but my tendency is to drop everything to please someone else. Life is a balancing act. Just as a toddler must learn to balance to walk, so too must I learn to balance so I can become me.

Today I will take my first toddler step toward learning how to balance my adaptability and my needs. I will let my feelings be mine and not worry about what others think or feel. Not bending to anyone's "you should feel," I will honor my feelings for what they are. I will attempt to strike a balance between what others want to do and what I want to do.

Just for today I will not be a "people pleaser;" instead I will do what is right for me.

Today I will leave old ways behind.

Today I will shed my old ways like a snake sheds its skin. I have been dragging these useless defenses around with me for so long that I don't even see them anymore. Yet others see them and they obscure the real me.

Now I will shake my old fears and negative attitudes loose and leave them behind. As a child, I needed them to survive. Now as I look at them, I am surprised at how dried up, thin and tattered they really are.

My new skin is smooth, shiny and alive. I move lightly, with delight. I am transformed. The face of my inner child is radiant.

I can be emotionally separate and still be caring.

I will not take on the anger, fear or moodiness of those around me today.

In my dysfunctional family, no one encouraged me to be a separate individual. When my parents were angry or depressed, I was made to feel that it was my fault. I was expected to *rescue* them emotionally. Well, taking on the rescuer role didn't work in childhood and it hasn't worked in my adult life, either. Because the source of others' unhappiness is inside them, nothing I can do will lift it from them. My detachment doesn't mean I don't care about their pain; it means that I know I cannot *save* them from their own moods.

I will honor my individuality today by refusing to take on the negative emotions of those around me.

I balance my work with relaxation.

I balance my work with relaxation, my reflection with activity. In this way I restore my productiveness and maintain sanity in my life.

When I was growing up, my dysfunctional family could not provide the structure that creates a balance between work and rest. I overachieved in an effort to win the approval of my parents, not realizing that they were not emotionally available for approval. Or, I may have given up and underachieved because I was afraid of failure. Both styles left me feeling incompetent or inadequate.

Today my inner child is bursting with activity. This child longs to be productive and useful. I will challenge my inner child with meaningful activity balanced with relaxation and reflection. I am restoring my inner child's spirit by creating balance in my life.

I affirm the truth of my recovery.

I fly to the moon on a motorcycle . . . My head was made in Brazil and my feet in Egypt . . . My mother is a trout, my father is a carp.

My inner child loves fantasies. In a certain way, the fantasy is true because it expresses a natural playfulness and a genuine wish.

As a child, I expressed a genuine desire to belong to a healthy family by fantasizing the ideal family: loving parents who took care of me, people who respected each other, a house filled with laughter and joy. As an adult child, I have fantasized that one day I would change my family. My understanding, my sensitivity and my goodness would compel my family members to face the truth and become healthy. Today I will honor the genuine desire of my inner child by differentiating fantasy from reality.

It is safe for my inner child to emerge.

The child within runs and hides when someone wants to come close. He lets himself be seen only for a short time, then gets frightened and runs away to hide again. He wants so much to be loved, to play, to experience the goodness of life. But life is too scary. Indeed, life has never been safe for him.

It is time to make life safe for my inner child and I have the power to create a safe haven. Safety brings freedom not only to accept and love myself but also to love others.

As I concentrate on making a safe haven for my inner child, I will be aware of my friends, old and new. I will choose friends who are emotionally healthy or moving on the journey toward wholeness. It is within the loving bonds of friendship that my inner child can come out and learn to feel safe.

I cultivate the needs of my inner child.

In nature, seeds can survive cold winters or long dry seasons. Ancient seeds have sprouted and flowered when thawed out and watered. As an adult in recovery, I have discovered beautiful old seeds that have survived my painful childhood. Each seed contains unfulfilled needs. At first, I did not know even their names; each one was small and dark, hard and closed. During my early days of recovery, the seeds began to sprout and I could differentiate a "feelings" seed from a "physical" seed, a "thinking" seed from a "spiritual" seed. Daily, as I tenderly care for my garden, I am fully aware that my inner child, too, needs structure and loving nourishment.

Today I will meet the needs of my inner child with precision. I will cultivate her growth with confidence and faith.

I can act on my ideas.

Today I affirm that I can act on my ideas. My ideas are worthy of exploration and action.

The creative spirit of my inner child comes up with all sorts of good ideas. They fill my mind like a bunch of gaily colored balloons. But cutting voices from my past often come to puncture them: "You could never do that; that's too hard. Someone else could do that much better than you can." Deflated and defeated, my good ideas disappear without a trace.

At this moment I acknowledge my creativity and my ability. I'm capable of so much more than I ever give myself credit for. Today I will take pleasure in figuring out how to implement my good ideas.

I will nourish myself in the right way.

Today I will give my inner child the nourishment she needs.

My parents controlled my eating. When I was good, food was a reward. When I was bad, I wasn't allowed to eat. In time, I got food all mixed up with my emotions. I could never tell if I was really hungry or if I needed emotional sustenance.

My inner child has a healthy appetite. Growing takes energy and spent energy needs to be replenished by food. I provide her with the right kinds of food — not too much sugar or fat, no stimulants or depressants, fresh fruits and vegetables, whole grains. I encourage her to pay attention to her body's messages — to eat as much as her body needs, to differentiate between physical and emotional hunger. When she's hungry for food, she can eat. When she's hungry for love, I give her as much as she can hold.

I can heal broken places in my soul.

Sometimes in the dark of night, the pain of unhealed wounds wells up inside me. I resent the past's intrusion into my present, so I struggle against the pain, pushing it deep within, in the hope that I will bury it once and for all. Unfortunately, the pain always returns. If the painful memories come tonight, I will wrap my arms around my little one within and hold her close. I will tell her that she is safe with me, that I understand her hurt as no one else but God does, that I know she didn't deserve the grief she's suffered. And I will reassure her that I will be the loving, attentive parent she never had. I visualize my innocent inner child cradled in my arms and I let my healing love flow from my body into hers. For her wounds are mine, a trust from God on behalf of one who cannot heal herself.

**My inner child is alive and
waiting to be healed.**

How do I discover my inner child? My capacity
to feel joy, to be spontaneous and take risks are
qualities that I was born with. These qualities
have not died, they are buried alive under years
of defenses and survival behaviors. My sincere
desire and firm decision to unlock my inner
child from despair is what will set me free.

The spirit of my inner child must be exercised
or she will wither away. I can no longer experience the wonder and glory of life by talking or
reading about it. I cannot bask in the warm
glow of someone else's inner child or live
through someone else's joy. I must live it myself.

I do not have to wonder where my inner child
is — she is inside of me waiting to show
herself, waiting to heal. Today I will put my
courage to work.

I use my power wisely.

In my family I learned about power. My parents were obsessed with their addiction and allowed me to manipulate them. Secretly I wanted limits but in my home there were none.

On the playground I pushed other kids around. I intimidated them into doing anything I wanted. On one hand, I liked the feeling of being able to control others. On the other, I was afraid and lonely. Bullies don't really have any friends. I was certain that someday my power would get out of hand and I would hurt myself or someone else.

Today I will make peace with my power. I can feel it radiate from deep within, strengthening my mind, my body and my soul. It is a force for me to use wisely. It can help me accomplish so many wonderful things.

In accepting that I am a powerful person, I can begin to see and respect the power in every person.

I can live in my body.

I loved my body when I was four years old. I used it to run, to jump rope, to climb trees. I continued to revel in it until I became a teenager. Then, suddenly, my body turned against me. It erupted in pimples, it grew in all the wrong places, I couldn't get my feet to go where I wanted them to go. I hated my body and after a while I hated myself for having the body I had. I hid it as best I could under loose, sloppy clothes. I slouched to make myself even more invisible. Soon I felt that no one could see my body and they couldn't see me, either. As the years passed, I grew tired of being invisible.

Now I am proud to be seen. I have thrown away the old clothes I used to hide behind. My new clothes express my personality and show my body off to its best advantage. My skin glows from the joy of having me back inside it. The four-year-old within me is happy that I have chosen to live inside my body again.

My recovery is taking shape!

When I was a child, my friends and I would spend hours and even days working on a jigsaw puzzle. At first, the pieces were a hopeless jumble of meaningless shapes and colors. Then, little by little, they began to take on meaning. This one was clearly an edge piece. That one must be a piece of sky. And that one surely was a part of a person's face! Piece by piece the pattern took shape. Then, suddenly, all the pieces fit together, the puzzle was solved.

Sometimes I get so caught up in what seems like meaningless details that I can't see the pattern of my life. During these times I get so frustrated that I want to give up on the whole process. When this happens, I remember my jigsaw puzzle days. I step back and really look at the pieces I have in my hands, as well as the pieces that others are adding to my life. Only then do I see my recovery taking shape.

Today I will live at a kinder pace.

My parents pushed me to read early, get good grades, work harder, go faster . . . Life was a race to the top of the ladder of success; the prize went only to the strongest. Play was a waste of time.

Well, I aimed for the top and I got there but I'm still running and I don't know how to stop. I'm moving so fast my life is a blur. I'm always under stress. I need to slow down.

Today I will live at a kinder pace. I turn off my alarm clock and sleep until my body tells me to wake up. I stretch and slowly get out of bed and stretch again. I ask myself, "What do I feel like doing today?" I wait for the answer. I'm surprised and delighted when it floats like a bubble into my mind.

With excitement, I begin to get ready for a new day.

**I am learning how to express
my anger responsibly.**

I will find appropriate outlets for my rage, neither ignoring it nor letting it control my life.

Before recovery, I believed anger was wrong so I channeled it in many unhealthy ways. All too often I vented my anger by using chemicals or food, abusing myself and others by my erratic, destructive behavior.

My parents taught me to believe that if I cut myself off from my rage, it would go away. Today I know that cutting myself off from my emotions keeps me from learning how to resolve them.

This is the day I will cease letting suppressed rage run my life. I will gently assist my child within to find responsible outlets for anger, rather than having tantrums. I will not unjustly direct my anger toward my partner, my children or my co-workers. Instead, I will turn to others for assistance and support.

I can determine what is right
and wrong for me.

Today begins a new chapter in my life. From now on, I will use the wisdom I have gained from my own successes and failures to determine what is right and wrong for me.

As a child, my parents and others of influence dictated their value systems to me. Unaware of my rights, I passively accepted their view of right and wrong as my own. Eventually, their expectations became a straitjacket that restricted my personal growth. Somewhere deep within I know that I am in danger of forever losing my integrity, my authenticity.

Today I will begin to affirm the decisions about right and wrong that come from the core of my own being, not from the opinions of others. I will experiment and discover what works best in my life without being paralyzed with the fear of making mistakes.

I am made of many parts.

When I was a child, I loved to take things apart and put them back together. The old percolator, broken watches, "Cootie" bug toys with six legs and two noses. It was endlessly fascinating to see how many different ways the same parts would fit together.

Today I am equally fascinated to discover my many facets. I look at myself piece by piece, exploring. How was this piece formed? Why is this piece broken? Can it be fixed? How does this part fit together with the others? If I put it back differently, will it still work?

I have learned that it is important not to rip myself apart in anger. I will not issue a death sentence to that little child inside who some-times shows herself as naughty, defiant or shameful. I delight in my ability to examine all my parts and then reassemble them with love, to make a fresh, new me.

**Today I will be patient with
my inner adolescent.**

A cacophony of sound assaults the ears as a symphony orchestra tunes their instruments. The disquieting bleats, screeches and bellows are quite unlike the harmonious and beautiful music to come. If patrons prejudged the scheduled performance solely by the tune-up, they would leave in a huff, never guessing the splendor of the music to follow.

Adolescence is like the tuning of a symphony orchestra. A whirlwind of emotions, decisions and actions creates distortion and confusion for adolescents and adults alike. It takes a good amount of patience to outlast the cacophony and await a beautiful symphony. Sometimes I am once again an adolescent, creating ugly, disjointed noises of my own. Too often I become discouraged by mistaking this confusion for the end result. Today I will see it as the tuning-up process, the preparation for a great symphony to come.

I can cry when I am sad or hurt.

My inner child lives in fear of being called a crybaby, of being considered weak. My parents often belittled my pain — "Oh come on, it can't be *that* bad!" — or denied it altogether — "You're just a crybaby. There's nothing wrong with you." I held my breath and made fists of my hands and drove the tears deep inside, where they remain to this day.

Today I embrace my inner child with love and allow myself to cry. My tears carry the old hurts from deep inside, coursing up until they spill over, pouring out, flowing freely. I feel the pain and hurt leaving my body as the tears wash away the misery and tension I have carried for so long.

I allow my inner child to cry and sob until no more tears come. I notice how much lighter I feel. I tell my inner child that whenever she is sad or hurt she can let her tears flow. It's okay to cry.

My inner child is the source of my vitality.

I will let my energy flourish today. I will pay attention to what I am feeling and express it.

The two-year-old within me needs to release emotions. This precious child had to curb all her vitality to be safe. Expressing anger, defiance or fear was often dangerous. All too often I had to hide from mother's disapproving eyes or father's violence. I thought if I really let my feelings show, my parents would leave and I would be alone.

Today my two-year-old is present and very much alive and I will love her the way she needs to be loved. This means that I can own my defiance and my stubbornness and not shame her. I will allow my inner child to heal by allowing myself to disagree with others. If I am in a dependent relationship, it is my two-year-old who will help me to separate. When I am taking a stand or stating a position, it is my precious little one who will give me the fuel to do it.

I am entitled to my own truth.

As a child I needed to distort my vision of truth in order to survive. When Dad was passed out on the floor from drinking, I held up my mental kaleidoscope and saw that he was napping. How could I have believed otherwise?

Unfortunately the distortion that allowed me to survive in childhood is destroying my adulthood. When I view life through my childhood lens, I don't see people for who they are and I stay in abusive situations.

Today I will put away my old kaleidoscope. I will view my relationships through the eyes of an adult and not the eyes of a frightened child. No longer will I lie to myself or anyone else. Living in fantasy is painful but gradually I am overcoming the obstacles that stand in the way of telling myself the truth.

I am the creator of my life.

Today I will affirm that I have the ability to create my own life. I no longer need to be shaped by the hands of people who do not have my best interests at heart. I no longer need to be merely the product of my dysfunctional upbringing. My inner child deserves better than that.

I am the clay and I am the sculptor. I can add a piece here, take away some there. I can build up areas that are weak, thin out areas that are dense and impenetrable. I can create an inner structure that allows me to be freestanding. The possibilities are endless.

I will never be finished creating myself. I am always in a state of becoming. With faith in my recovery process and trust in my Higher Power, I am creating a new me.

Today my inner child skips for joy.

Today the child within me skips for joy but only a few weeks ago, my inner child was struggling with the rhythm: one-two-three, one-two-three, heel-toe-step, heel-toe-step. My feet wanted to run away or hop wildly, as if saying, "You only have two of us, and we go one-two, one-two. That's all we can do. That's all we can do."

Yet deep inside, I felt another rhythm — graceful as a dance and clever as a riddle. So I persevered and one day my feet put a hop and a run together one-two-three and I skipped perfectly. The next day my feet got tangled and I had to start over again. And soon my feet were skipping without me telling them to.

Today I feel the joy of living, which my hard work has made easy. I look back over my struggles and marvel at how far I have come.

Today I will say no without guilt.

Today I will say no whenever it is in my best interests to do so. Just as important, I will say no without feeling guilty or fearful.

My attempts to separate from my parents were met with threats of abandonment. As a result, I learned to avoid having my own opinion for fear of rejection.

Deep within me now, I feel a strong desire to become my own person, to stand free of all unhealthy attachments and discover who I am. When I disregard my limitations and permit others to violate my boundaries, I harm myself.

Today I will love myself enough to say no when I find it necessary. I will reassure the child within me that those who truly love me will not abandon me when I must tell them no. No matter what the response, today I will treat myself well by saying no without guilt and fear.

I am lovable at every age.

I am lovable at any age. I do not have to know more than I know, feel differently than I feel or look and act a certain way. My being is lovable and I am loved for myself.

Sometimes children try out behaviors that are less or more mature than their age. A four-year-old who wants to be cuddled like an infant may act babyish. A six-year-old who wants companionship may ask grown-up questions to engage the attention of an adult. In my dysfunctional family, I was ridiculed for immature or precocious behavior. I got my needs met by acting "grown-up" or staying little. I never had permission to act my age, so I never learned what that meant. I did not learn that I was loved no matter what my stage of growth.

Today I will love the child within me and I love my adult self. I will get my needs met by asking directly for affection or companionship. I am lovable at any age and I deserve to be loved.

Today my inner child is free from fear.

I am simply on this earth
Need I be afraid?
Mandan chant, translated by Frances Densmore

I observe the small child who is tossed into the air and, all smiles and laughter, falls into the strong, outstretched arms of a loving parent. The child is both secure and adventurous.

Today I will release my fears and worries into the care of my Higher Power. Doing so will leave me free to explore the world about me and the life within me.

I can examine my feelings in safety. I can stretch my body and touch a delicate blossom, trace an ironwork railing, skip rocks across a pond. I can explore my spirituality and envision a Higher Power who desires my growth.

Today I will be free from fear and free to explore.

I allow my curiosity to emerge.

My curiosity is alive today as I set out to explore places that pique my interest. It is my curiosity that propels me to learn more about my world.

Between six and 18 months of age, our internal clocks inspire curiosity, urging us to explore our world. When I was a toddler, however, my curiosity was not validated. My parents were quick to say, "Stop that!" "Don't touch this!" "No, you can't!" Too often I was spanked or humiliated for acting my age. So whenever my inner child shyly extends a hand out to the world, I do not slap it and scold this precious one. Instead I affirm her right and her courage to express her curiosity.

Today, if I am curious, I will explore physically, mentally and emotionally. I will explore through conversation and investigation. If I am puzzled by something, I will ask for an explanation. My toddler within is safe today and happy to be taken care of.

My ideals are part of my reality.

My ideals are an intrinsic part of my human-ness. I do not choose whether to have ideals or not, just as I do not choose whether I am human or not. Rather, I choose ideals that reflect my personal values.

When I expressed lofty dreams and goals as a child, various adults in my life said, "You're young and idealistic. Wait till you grow up." If growing up meant sacrificing my personal dreams or my desire for justice in the world, I did not want to grow up.

Today I announce the good news to my inner child: I will never lose my idealism. Idealism is a part of being human and being human is a part of reality.

Throughout my recovery and maturity, I will commit to identifying ideals that reflect my desires and values. I will seek out groups and organizations that effectively translate ideals into action. Through word and deed, I will fulfill my ideals.

I will listen to words today.

Words bring the world to children.

Words shape the world: circles, triangles, squares, straight lines and curves.

Words color the world: magenta, black, canary yellow.

Words make sense: explain, learn, show.

Words make nonsense: cuckoo, pink elephants, how's them potatoes.

Words celebrate: glitter, party, Christmas.

Words open: window, imagination, change.

Words bring joy: sing, dance, laugh, play.

Words bring messages to adults: heal, empower, grow, today.

I trust myself.

My inner child does not trust herself to cross the street without being hit by a car or to walk on a mountain path without falling off a ledge. The committee inside her head says, "You can't do that. You're too little, clumsy, too dumb." She reaches out for hands to hold, expecting others to steady her step. Once again, there are no hands to count on. She freezes, frightened to move on her own.

Today I will take myself into my own hands, confident in their strength and capability. I will remain calm and listen to my inner wisdom, the voice that says, "Go ahead, I trust you. You'll be fine." I walk hand in hand with my inner child until she is ready to let go.

I encourage my toddler's efforts to walk.

I watch my toddler take her first steps. I want to rush to her aid and show her the best way to keep from hurting herself.

When I was a toddler, there was not enough protection for me. There was little opportunity to explore and I was pushed to organize and think about my world too soon. Perhaps as a parent, I have compensated because of my own lack of nurturing.

Today I realize that if I keep my child from her pain, she will never learn to resolve her emotions. I must allow her to make mistakes so that she can find out what works best for *her*. I must let her fall so that she can learn to pick herself up. I will not take away her right to feel courageous and proud and powerful.

What I can offer my child is what I always wanted . . . an environment that is safe, a parent who is loving and encouraging and a hand to hold.

I am creating a healthy future.

Snow drifts to the ground in soft white flakes, changing the shape and the look of the land. When the snow is thick and deep, it hides everything, both beautiful and ugly. Abandoned cars, garbage, flowers and gardens become vague shapes in the fields of endless white. It is not until spring that we really know what lies beneath the snow. I have buried my past underneath many feet of snow. This beautiful cover hides the good and the bad alike. New growth and new healing cannot take place until spring comes.

Today I will no longer be afraid of spring. I will welcome it. When my past is revealed, I will remove the old debris and reflect on the good memories there. Then, like a loving gardener, I will plant seeds, encouraging new growth. In this season of rebirth I am creating a healthy future by tending to my recovery.

My inner child rejoices today.

When I was a child, I had to neglect my own needs in order to survive in my family. Oftentimes my bodily functions were ignored out of fear.

There were nights when I had to lie in bed listening to alcoholic arguments, afraid to go to the bathroom. I learned to hold my breath during violent episodes at home in order not to feel anything. My mind remained on mental alert 24 hours a day but my body longed for rest.

As an adult, I still suffer from childhood wounds. In an effort to shut out pain, I take short gasps of air barely filling my lungs. Frequently, I get so busy that I literally forget to eat or even go to the bathroom.

Today I will commit myself to three basic tasks that mark a new beginning: I will breathe, I will feel, I will relax.

I will radiate a passion of delight.

I affirm the healing quality of laughter and every day I catch funny glimpses of life, jokes, slips of the tongue and bizarre ironies.

I can smile, I can laugh at my own pretensions. I can be unserious and clown and walk like a horse. Laughter works like Drano to cleanse the emotional pipes of backed-up sludge. Laughter drains the body of tension and leaves it as limp as a strand of boiled spaghetti. Laughter makes my soul vibrate with joy.

There are times when sadness, intense pain and anger smother the mirth and make life seem bleak and humorless. Yet, thanks to that magical child within, I have the power to summon a smile and notice the comical incongruities that come each day. Today I will open my mind to life's mirth and gaiety and I will let my smile truly radiate a passion of delight.

Today I will reclaim my body.

As a child, my body was everyone's property — everyone's except mine. Others could touch it whenever and however they pleased and no one could stop them, least of all me. As far as I knew, abuse was love. My only defense was to deny that my body was part of me.

For far too long I have continued to let anyone and everyone abuse my body — usually in the name of love. Today it stops. My body belongs to me. No one has the right to tell me what to do with it. It's up to me to decide when and how I want to be touched and when I do not feel like being touched. My body contains myself. I must keep it strong and healthy and treat it with respect and I expect others to respect my body as I do.

Today I will reclaim my body. I am developing healthy, physical boundaries for my own sake and that of my inner child.

It's important to find what pleases me.

As a baby, it was important to squirm to find the most comfortable position. Through struggling, each of us learns to physically bond with others. But many of us were raised by parents who were addicts that became impatient with our squirming. Some of us were raised with narcissistic parents who interpreted our squirming as an insult — that the child doesn't want to be held at all. So we learned quite early to adjust our behavior to please our parents. In my adulthood there still exists an infant who longs for bonding. When I am hugged or embraced, I become stiff and unyielding. If I'm uncomfortable I stay quiet.

Today when I am touched or hugged by someone I trust, I will squirm and struggle all I want until I am comfortable. I will tell my inner child that, "It's okay to find out what pleases you." It's important for me to find my place with others.

Today I summon my adolescent energy.

Pacing restlessly — Never at rest,
Never at peace. Lurking and waiting
Like a panther in a cage.

— Greg Spieker

As an adolescent, I savored freedom like a whiff of a strong, sweet odor that I could almost taste. Yet I was overwhelmed by choices and possibilities.

By the time I was a teenager, I could summon dreams and visions easily but I still believed that ideas alone could change the world. No one ever taught me how to connect ideas to action.

In my early recovery, I glimpsed a vision of a free and healthy life that felt so real I thought I could touch it. As I grew in wisdom, I learned that freedom, like my recovery, proceeds day by day. Today I will summon the energy of my adolescent panther and step closer to my vision of freedom.

> I am pleased with my physical
> and spiritual vision.

As a teenager, grooming was an intense activity. As a boy, I agonized for hours while shaving three whiskers. As a girl, I applied mascara as if performing delicate eye surgery. When I looked into a mirror I sought perfection; understandably I was often disappointed. Then one day I glimpsed a vision that was more than attractive; I saw a face that did not belong to any other man or woman and I began to claim my physical uniqueness as beauty. Sometimes the vision was clouded over by peer pressure or a culture that narrowly defines beauty. As an adult child, I forget that I ever saw a vision of my face that pleased me.

Today I will look in the mirror and rediscover my uniqueness. I will observe the changes in my face that recovery has shaped. As I recover, my face reflects inner strength and integrity and I am pleased with both my physical and spiritual vision.

**Today I will take advantage of
the resources at hand.**

A story is told of a man who was marooned on
the roof of his house during a flood. As various
vehicles passed and the people inside offered
him a lift to safety, his inner child's magical
thinking found voice and stated, "God will
rescue me." The man eventually perished in
the flood. When he came face to face with God,
the man demanded to know why God had not
rescued him. God answered, "Well, I sent you
a raft, a rowboat, a motorboat and a helicopter."

My scared inner child does not need to wait to
be saved by magic. I will no longer blame
others or martyr myself. I will take decisive
action based on the vehicles available to me
now. My sense of purpose and well-thought-
out decisions will take me to safety. My Higher
Power may send opportunities for healing and
growth my way but it is up to me to take advantage of the resources at hand. Today I will take
responsibility for my healing.

Today I feel the stirring of new life within me.

Natalie Goldberg writes about a teacher who called her aside one day and said: "Look under the desks. There's mud on the floor from their shoes. That's a good sign. It means spring."

Transitions are not tidy. In early spring, winter still lingers. When the blanket of snow is finally stripped from the ground, brown grass and muddy sidewalks appear. But new life is stirring and the ends of bare branches are tipped with small hard buds.

In early spring I feel restless and vaguely uncomfortable. But I am preparing for change and the discomfort I feel is giving way to new growth. In my dysfunctional family, I felt constant discomfort. I had no stability with which to measure or predict change. Today I will welcome messiness and equate restlessness with a kind of excitement. I feel secure in the working of my Higher Power. My potential is unfolding and I feel new life stirring within me.

Loving touch heals the child within.

Touch energizes. Touch heals. Touch creates a sense that the world is not just a bad or scary place. Touch says someone cares that I'm alive.

In my childhood home, loving touch was rare. It often came only when my needs were too great to be denied any longer. Worse, touch did not necessarily mean love, it often came with anger. Now in my adulthood, it isn't easy for me to be comfortable with being touched.

Today I will arrange to have a massage, whether performed by a professional or a close friend. I will allow myself to relax, letting the energy flow into my body. I will still my mind so no thoughts will interrupt my pleasure. Through touch, I will allow myself to feel safe, loved and cared for.

I choose to have positive thoughts.

Negative beliefs and attitudes from my family of origin limit my opportunities and stifle my emotions. These attitudes contaminate and undermine my personal and professional adult life.

I acknowledge that I possess emotions but I am so much more than my emotions. Although my emotions and thoughts can flow through my consciousness, I do not have to be swept away by them.

Today I will not allow negative beliefs to dominate my thoughts. I will carefully select only healthy thoughts to guide my actions. If unhealthy beliefs crop up, I will bid them adieu like house guests who have outstayed their welcome.

I will greet my feelings like old and dear friends who want to visit for a while and then depart.

My sexuality belongs to me.

Feeling sexual is part of how I am made, what I am created to feel. Feeling sexual is not wrong. Just because I feel sexual doesn't mean I have to act on it. I can feel sexual and still be responsible for my sexuality. Feeling is *not* the same as acting.

If my feelings seem to threaten or overwhelm me, I will quiet the turmoil by treating myself with gentleness. I will give voice to my inner adolescent who is learning how to deal with sexuality.

I am in charge of myself. I will allow no one else to tell me what to do, manipulate me into doing something I don't want to do or ridicule me for my choices. My sexuality belongs to me and only me. It is a gift. And I can share it with whomever I choose.

I will rejoice in my sexuality this day.

Restfulness fills every part of my being.

Tonight I need desperately to rest, to let go of churning thoughts and relax knotted muscles. But bands of steel seem to hold my body rigid. Scenes from my childhood flicker behind my closed eyes: screaming arguments between parents whose violent words filled me with terror. The terrified five-year-old within me warns, "Protect yourself! The world is dangerous. You have to stay alert!" My child within needs to be loved, to be comforted. In my thoughts, I cradle her in my arms, press her cheek close to mine, and gently rub the knotted muscles in her neck and back until the viselike grip of tension and fear is released.

And now in my mind's eye, a warm pool of light, glowing with love and safety, surrounds us both. With joy, I realize that as I have comforted this little one within, so too have I released my adult burdens. A deep restfulness fills every part of my being.

The child within me is worthy of love.

A huge stuffed rabbit named Alex sits on my bed. Alex has the distinct privilege of sitting in for my inner child whenever necessary. When the little child within me needs to be comforted, I cradle Alex in my arms and rock him. When my inner child needs a soothing lullaby, I softly sing to Alex. I treat Alex in ways I wish I had been treated as a little one.

Today I will find ways to nurture my inner child. There are many ways I can coax my little one out of hiding. I can buy a book of simple songs and lullabies to sing to my inner child. I can caress away all fear and anxiety with gentle words and melodies.

In my mind's eye, I will rock my inner child and whisper sweet and silly messages in his ear. He is special and wonderful, worthy of all the love I can give. Today he will be filled with my love.

I express my emerging personality.

My inner child is a gifted actor. Throughout the day I am able to adjust to the many facets of my life. I may be nurturing, competent, silly, serious or sexy. I portray many roles adeptly and celebrate my own diversity. I convince myself that I am one character and then I shed one costume for another and blink my eyes at the sudden transformation.

I know who I am and I endlessly surprise myself. I expect surprises to be a part of my growth and I delight in my changes.

In recovery, I discover new ways to express my emerging personality. I exercise my growing powers with new roles and new ways of being.

My body is a miracle.

Look at me! Look at me! My inner child demands that I pay attention to the wonderful way my body responds.

My body is not a briefcase that waits patiently by the door until I am ready to go to work. My body is a miracle and, therefore, I am. My body is a mystery and I am endlessly fascinated by its inner and outer workings.

Today I observe my body in action. I cross the street and marvel at my eyes and ears that are alert to danger as well as beauty. I am aware of my legs that move me from place to place. Even my skin responds to the breeze as it flows against my face. I breathe deeply and marvel at the constant renewing of my body and spirit.

My body's wisdom and authority fill me with awe and deep comfort.

I am healing from the inside out.

As a child of an alcoholic, I tend to view God in the same way I viewed my parents: as violent, capricious, critical and judgmental. I grew up with the notion that I had to do a lot of begging and praying just to be heard. I truly believed that if I was not perfect, I would be punished. I grew up spiritually bankrupt. I experienced a vast emptiness that cried to be filled up. In my desperation, I turned to food, drugs, sex and relationships to provide me with a sense of completeness. After years of pain, I realized that there was no quick fix.

Today I realize that co-dependency is, in part, a spiritual illness that needs to be healed from the inside out. In recovery I find spirituality stems from self-love. As I learn to reparent my inner child, I slowly begin to experience the God-like qualities of joy, beauty, freedom and unconditional love. Now I have faith that I am well on my way to wholeness.

I can dress like an adult and still be me.

It seems like I've been wearing blue jeans forever. As a young teenager, I soon learned that jeans were a badge of belonging, a satisfyingly simple rebellion against my parents who wanted me to wear "proper" clothes. Decked out in my jeans, I was accepted by my friends, I fit in and I gently thumbed my nose at convention.

My teenaged years passed but I continued to wear blue jeans every day. I felt uncomfortable in other kinds of clothes. I just didn't feel like myself without my blue jeans.

Today I am no longer a rebellious teenager. I am comfortable in my maturity. I dress appropriately for the situation. At work I wear work clothes; for parties I dress up. When it feels right, I wear blue jeans. I can dress like a grown-up and still be me. My freedom with clothes reflects my inner freedom.

I feel and express my true feelings.

In recovery, I seek safe places and appropriate ways for the child within me to express powerful emotions.

While I was growing up, my parents did not express their feelings in clear and responsible ways. I learned to hide or mislabel my emotions. I felt anger when I was scared and sadness when I was angry.

In recovery, I am learning to express my feelings honestly. If I am angry with a friend, I express my feelings with an angry tone of voice and I describe their behavior and my feelings without blaming. If I am angry with someone I do not trust, I express my feelings privately. If I am sad, I may phone a friend and ask for comfort or I may play sad music and cry as long as I need to. If I am happy, I may smile broadly or laugh aloud.

Today I will feel my true feelings and express them appropriately.

My imagination is alive and well.

Let's pretend . . . I can be anyone I want to be. When I allow my inner child to use her imagination, I can free myself of my negative and hurtful misconceptions about myself.

I wish I were . . . a strong, decisive person. And, presto, I am! In my mind's eye, I stand tall and proud. I know my own mind, and it feels great.

I wish I were . . . happy more of the time. I pretend to be happy and feel a smile light up my face. The act of smiling turns on a faucet of happiness in my body. Children learn by experimenting with new behaviors. Pretending to be different than I usually am allows me to "try on" unfamiliar but coveted attributes — like strength, decisiveness, happiness.

Today I will use my imagination to create new patterns for living.

I am connected to the earth.

In adolescence I was clumsy and uncoordinated. I couldn't make the bat hit the ball. I tripped over my own feet. The physical world was no longer safe for me so I took refuge inside my head, where I could be in control.

Without ever realizing it, my head became not a refuge but a home. I wanted to escape my body and, in doing so, I became completely unaware of myself in the world. As a result, I am not rooted in reality, I cannot take in cues from my environment and I feel no sense of grounding or support.

Today, with each step, I will plant my feet firmly on the ground. I will feel the energy from deep inside the earth radiate upward through the soles of my feet and spread the earth's energy throughout my body. Like an umbilical cord, the earth's energy connects me gently but securely to the source of life. I will not float away. I am connected to the earth.

I belong in the world as I am.

I walk down the slope of beach, leaving behind cars in the parking lot, grass and rock on land. My feet sink into sand and I slow down. I walk to the water's edge; a wave laps at my toes. I chase it back into the ocean and for a few moments the waves and I play tag.

Then I notice my footprint — the hollow impression of my heel and the spreading fan of toes. The waves wash up upon the shore and fill my print with water. I name my worries, my fears in every speck of sand. Grain by grain, my footprint is washed away.

The waves roll into shore again and I release my responsibilities and my concerns into the care of the ocean. The shore is smooth and gleaming. My mind is at peace. The water provides a lullaby that is soothing and relaxing. I look toward the horizon and blue fills my eyes. I am part of nature and I belong in the world as I am.

I know who I am.

Who am I?

Am I the person my parents wanted me to be? Am I who my friends think I am? Am I the face I present to the world?

Sometimes I feel like a crowd — I can become a different person at anytime for anyone. No wonder it's so easy for me to lose track of myself.

At this moment I still my many personalities and listen to my inner voice. Its clear, calm tone fills me with certainty. My many faces are expressions of my true self. I know who I am.

I bring honesty to my relationships.

As a child I was deathly afraid to be honest. Terrorized by the raging of parents as well as emotional and physical abuse, I learned very early that it was useless and sometimes dangerous to express my needs directly. I became adept at whining and complaining.

As an adult I refined my childhood pattern to perfection. I manipulated others into nurturing me by looking hopelessly needy or helpless or by appearing to be in crisis or on the brink of disaster. In reality, my dishonesty served to push others away and to erode my own sense of integrity and worth.

Today I will share openly with others what I feel and what I need. No game-playing manipulation, no strings attached. Whatever the response, I will have the deep satisfaction of knowing that I have taken a significant step forward on my journey to wholeness.

I deserve order and beauty in my life.

Chores for children: "You can't play outside until you finish vacuuming. You can't go to the movies until the leaves are raked."

Like many other children and adults, I dread the word *chores*. I associate chores with the absence of fun. Often household tasks were used to punish me. My parents neglected to teach me household skills and I still feel incompetent in managing my daily tasks.

Today I will enjoy doing one chore. I will choose a task I actually enjoy or find a way to make my work fun. Loud and lively music, with pauses for dancing, may make mopping the kitchen floor a pleasure. Today I acknowledge my competence as an adult; I deserve the order and beauty of a well-maintained household.

I can swim in the waters of life.

Today I will affirm my ability to swim through the waters of life.

Sometimes I feel as if I am caught in a flood — of emotions, fears, possibilities. I feel as if I will be swept away by the onrushing tide of life. I am in awe — and fear — of the size of the wave rushing toward me. Like a child at the beach for the first time, if I stand here and let myself be overwhelmed by life, I will drown. If I leap in and swim with the tide, I can save myself.

This is not my first day at the beach, however, and I know how to swim. So I leap into the water and swim with strong, confident strokes. I allow the tide to carry me along as I make my own way. When I tire, I rest for a moment, treading water, watching the never ending flow of life. When I'm rested, I take a breath and keep swimming.

**I will greet this new day with
anticipation and excitement.**

Sometimes the day weighs heavily upon me as I lie in bed at night. It is difficult to sleep as I reflect back over the day. Each mistake and each problem looms large in my head. I wonder whether I can face another day.

The morning dawns, giving birth to a new day, giving birth to a new supply of energy that will be just enough for today. If I focus only on the present, I don't need to fear the future. I will have enough energy to face whatever problems wait for me there.

Each new day brings opportunity to start over, to leave behind the mistakes I've made. If I've failed, if I've made wrong choices, I will say the apologies that need to be said and move on.

My soul is refreshed by the sun and the promise of a brand new day. Like my gleeful inner child, I will greet this day with anticipation and excitement.

My sensuality is awakened by nature.

As a child, nature held unfolding surprises. Each season brought new sights, new smells, new sounds and new activities. As an adult, I have two basic responses to the changing of seasons: "It's too cold, turn on the heat" or "It's too warm, turn on the air conditioning." I have shut out the messages of the seasons. In doing so, I have also cut myself off from the continual changes of my world. I have forgotten the joy I felt as a child at the turn of the seasons: leaping into the crisp brown leaves of fall, cooling off in the sprinklers under the hot sun of summer, the sun's glare bouncing off fresh snow, the smell of grass being mown in spring.

Today I will open my senses — to the warm sun heating up my skin, to the cool nip of wind blowing through my hair, to the smell of rain on a hot pavement, to the cold night air filling my lungs. My attention to my senses gives my life a sharp new intensity.

> **When I release my innocence,
> I accept my wisdom.**

Coming of age means losing my innocence. I must release my innocence as a necessary part of my growth. By doing so, I do not lose my goodness or my idealism. Both my goodness and idealism are rooted in wisdom.

I may mourn the loss of innocence but my deepest sorrow comes from the fact my innocence was betrayed. I grew up in a family system ruled by the effects of compulsive or abusive behavior. I accepted those rules in innocence. I granted their importance out of my inherent love and trust for my parents. Today, if the time is right, I will honor my innocence by releasing it. My innocence served my inner child until my knowledge and judgment could protect us both. As I release my innocence, I accept my wisdom.

Today I will renounce my perfectionism.

Today I will renounce my perfectionism and lovingly embrace all of who I am.

As a child, I earned my right to exist by being perfect. In my dysfunctional family, mistakes were simply not acceptable. Over and over, however, perfection proved to be an unattainable goal. The mistakes and failures that come with being human constantly mocked me. Most damaging of all, my perfectionism drove me to try to be someone I am not.

As part of my recovery, I have discovered that there is something incredibly freeing about acknowledging that I am a combination of strengths and limitations.

Today I will love and respect the frightened child within me who had to be perfect to be acceptable. Today I will celebrate my humanness and the qualities that make me who I am.

I am the advocate for my inner child.

Today I am my inner child's advocate. I patiently await the expression of that child's feelings and needs. The more intently I listen, the more eloquently the child within me speaks. The more I give voice to my child self, the better I take care of myself.

I felt lost as a child in my dysfunctional family. I felt adult pressures that mutilated my inner child. There was no room for my needs or perspective. There was no room to be a child.

Today there is room in my life for both the child self and the adult self. I add spontaneity and structure to my life by negotiating the needs of my child self and the responsibilities of my adult self. My world is rich and full and all my feelings belong.

I can give sexual pleasure to myself.

I can give sexual pleasure to myself. I am the lover of my own body. When I know how to love myself sexually, I will know how it feels to be properly loved.

As a child and adolescent, I felt deep shame about my sexual needs. Touching myself was a sin; something was definitely wrong with me if I wanted to do "that sort of thing." The un-named pleasure was forever out of my grasp. I was denied the knowledge — and the joy — of my own body.

Today I will affirm my right to give sexual pleasure to myself. I will allow myself to explore all my nooks and crannies, to get to know myself on this erotic plane. When I know myself sexually, I can share my knowledge with others to create successful sexual relationships.

I am responsible for my happiness.

I will be responsible for my own happiness today by identifying and naming my pain.

The unspoken rules in my alcoholic family were, "Don't feel. Don't talk." Other than anger, feelings were not expressed. This encouraged me to bury my feelings deep inside and to deny their existence. Even now as an adult, I often feel unhappy but I don't know why. Sometimes when I'm hurting and that knife-edge of emotional pain wells up inside, I remain confused and unable to identify what it is.

Today, when pain wells up from the dark places in my soul, I will seek to name it. Is it fear? Is it worry? Is it anger? What am I feeling?

I will gently probe the dimensions of my pain today and I will name it. In naming it, I will feel the quiet joy of knowing that I have taken an important new step toward being responsible for my own happiness.

I can be tenacious, not stubborn.

Today I know the difference between stubbornness and tenacity.

When I was a child, I would hold onto a whim no matter how silly, selfish or dangerous it was. Unwilling, or unable, to let go, I would lock my jaws like a pit bull and vow to hold on till the death, even if it was my own death.

To hold on because I have too much pride to let go is stubbornness and it's a dead end. To hold on because I have faith I'll succeed, despite adversity and obstacles, is tenacity. With no effort at all I can take the pointless self-destructive power of stubbornness and transform it into the positive power of tenacity. I need to be courageous and persistent to handle the difficulties life brings.

I marvel at my growth and healing.

Children are constantly amazed by their growth. They look at booties they wore as infants and they feel as huge and as different as dinosaurs. They look at old yellowing school papers they printed in first grade; they try to trace the big block letters, but their facile fingers cannot move in the old awkward ways.

The child within me grows in leaps and bounds. Indeed, sometimes I do not recognize my inner child from one day to the next because the growth seems dramatic and sudden.

I have learned in recovery to be patient and allow myself time to heal. Some days I notice my serenity or my detachment and I shake my head like a child who cannot believe he used to wear the tiny T-shirt. Today I will take stock of my growth, I will marvel with my inner child at how far we have come.

Gradually I am learning to trust and love.

I'm afraid to let you love me. My whole inner being shouts, "Please don't love me. I don't want to be hurt again!" Loving means hurting. Love means pain. Love means broken promises, lies and sarcasm.

At least that's what love meant in my family of origin. It doesn't have to mean that today.

Cats pause by an open door, tails swishing. They lift their ears high, fully alert, gauging how safe it is beyond the door. In a flash, they bolt through the door. Sometimes that is how I respond to love.

Today I will approach love with caution; I will not throw myself headlong into it. Little by little, I will open myself up to someone of value, someone I can trust with a small portion of myself. I will let someone love me, knowing I am worthy of that love.

Today I choose to think before I act.

I have an excellent mind and today I will choose to think instead of acting childish to accomplish my goals in life. As a child, I received lots of attention and praise for acting cute. I wasn't praised for thinking because my co-dependent parents wanted to do my thinking for me. They preferred the cute act because it kept me in the role of their little boy. So, I learned to play the role well.

Indeed, I learned it so well that I still act cute to get my way as an adult. On the inside, however, I don't feel cute. When I peel away the layers of charm, I feel inadequate and shameful.

Today I feel a stirring within me, a new desire to use my mind to achieve my goals. It is time for me to grow up. I no longer have to entertain others to feel good about myself. I will reassure my charming inner child that I can meet his needs in other ways. Today I will choose to think rather than act cute to get what I need in life.

**My inner child is alive with the
newness of spring.**

Today I feel the wild, generative energy of life
pulsing within. The green, growing springtime
energy is coursing through my bloodstream.
Each cell of my body is bursting, expanding. I
hear music in the sounds of the street. The
colors of life fill my eyes with their brilliance.
Flowers call out to me, asking me to celebrate
the glory of life with them.

I feel like dancing, laughing, singing my joy to
the world. The child within me is bursting free,
glad to be alive. I welcome my inner child with
open arms. Today we will dance to life together.

I will teach my inner child about support.

My parents were always too busy holding their own chaotic lives together. Because I never had anyone but myself to depend on during my childhood, I've learned to trust no one. It's a difficult, lonely way to live.

Today I will teach my inner child how it feels to lean on others for support. I stand up straight, close my eyes and imagine sunlight pouring over me. My jaw muscles loosen and my face goes slack. What a relief to let go of my frozen expression. Slowly, my neck relaxes and my head tilts forward. With my eyes still closed, I feel my shoulders droop, my spine unstiffening. I feel like a limp noodle. My legs begin to wobble; I need to sit in a chair or lean against a wall. I relax fully, knowing I will not fall. I trust my support to keep me from crashing to the floor. Now my inner child and I know how it will feel to have friends who will gladly help me. Now I know I can lean on others for support.

Today I create a new childhood.

If I could have chosen my childhood, I would not have chosen the one I had. I have allowed myself to grieve the loss of what was rightfully mine. Now I must take a new direction, one that leads me away from the past.

It is time for me to choose a new childhood. What did I long to do as a child? Take dance lessons? Go to the amusement park and buy balloons and cotton candy? Stare at the animals in the zoo? Ride a merry-go-round? All the things I wanted to experience can now be part of my activities and memories. Maybe I'll invite a friend who also enjoys being a child to play with me.

It is time to make happy memories for my inner child. Today I will do at least one enjoyable thing that the child within me never had the freedom to do.

Today I let go of my unhealthy anger.

Today I will stop using anger to punish and
control. The anger I feel over the losses and
undeserved hurts of my childhood is appropriate. However, on my journey toward wholeness, I must own the anger that seethes and
erupts out of my own unhealthy places. Sometimes I feel this anger when others fail to meet
my needs. In recovery, I have come to see that
meeting my needs is my own responsibility.

At other times, I use this anger as punishment, a
whip to get my way. The child within me reacts
this way when cornered and powerless. Yet, this
anger violates my own standards of conduct.

Today I know that I no longer need to use this
unhealthy form of anger. Far from being helpless, I now know that I am powerful.

Today I will leave behind my inappropriate
anger and move ahead with quiet confidence
and peace.

**My inner child is free to grow and
I am free to heal.**

A Jewish saying goes, "In remembrance is the secret of redemption." Remembering is a testament to surviving; only survivors remember. Memory is also the opportunity to heal and to recover.

Memories are painful, not so much because the experience was painful, but because the denial was painful. To survive painful experiences while growing up, I denied myself my feelings, my perceptions and my reality. The greatest pain was loss of myself.

In remembering, I do not deny myself anymore. I experience the feelings of my inner child and my inner child is free to heal.

Today I will welcome my memories as opportunities to grow. In remembering, I will transform my survival into recovery.

Today I will let my inner child explore.

Don't! Don't touch! Don't get too close! Don't feel! In sheer frustration this toddler begins to yell. She only wants to express her healthy anger at not being allowed to do what comes naturally to her. A slap and then a scolding voice assails her until she stops.

Her world is fascinating and inviting. She wants to do, not think. What's that soft furry creature? What's that shiny pretty thing on the table? And what could be on the other side of that wall or down the street? Yet, fences trap her on all sides; verbal fences, fences of raised eyebrows, wood fences, fences of soft netting.

Today I will let the toddler within me explore. I will feel a flower and hear the sound it makes when pulled from its stem, eat something new, touch something that has beckoned for so long. I will no longer inhibit the child within who wants to explore the world. At the same time, I will be wise and keep her from danger, encouraging her to experience what is safe.

I am aware of the consequences
of my actions.

I am all too aware of how other people's actions affect me. Yet whenever I am brave enough to ask others how my actions made them feel, I am often surprised to find out that words I meant in jest were received in pain, that actions I meant as thoughtful were taken as put-downs. Clearly, I need to examine my motives, to pay closer attention to what I am doing.

My words and actions affect everyone around me. A rock dropped into a pond sends out concentric waves that grow wider and wider until they fill the entire pond. Similarly, my actions have an effect that reaches far beyond me. Today I will pay attention to how my actions affect others.

Today I will take care of me.

For as long as I can remember, I have lived my life for others. Pleasing others was of utmost importance in my struggle to protect my emotional and physical well-being.

As an adult child, I lived my life for others in an attempt to gain their approval and their love. I consistently put others' needs and preferences ahead of my own.

Now I know that living my life solely to please others is nothing more than a form of slow emotional starvation. Like any addiction, my enslavement to others' approval demands that I give up more and more of myself and take less and less in return.

Today I will begin to recover from my addiction to others' approval. I will consider my own needs, desires and preferences first. Today I will take care of me.

I stand by my inner child today.

My inner child is afraid of bullies. It never seems to fail. Just as the game gets going, a bully steps in to ruin it — pushing kids around, making up the rules, threatening to tell about some unknown crime.

As a child, I surrendered my sense of power to bullies who always seemed so much bigger and stronger. I hated it but I didn't know what else to do. I was afraid.

Today I will help my inner child deal with bullies. As an adult, I can see bullies for what they are: sad, angry children who want to play with others but don't know how unless they can push others around. I will stand by my inner child whatever the game and help her stand up for herself. We can't change how bullies act but we can change our reactions to them.

I know that I can succeed.

Today I will look at my tasks with the eyes of an adult and not the eyes of a child. I will not allow my rebellious inner child to interfere with the work that I must accomplish today. I will firmly prod my inner adolescent who wants to procrastinate and complain. I will calm my inner child who feels helpless in carrying out adult responsibilities.

Doing inner child work does not mean that the child must take over. It would be ridiculous to expect my 13-year-old to drive me to work, conduct a meeting or negotiate a business deal. There are times that I must fulfill commitments and meet deadlines. During these times I depend upon my adult wisdom balanced by my child's creativity. This day I will enter new projects with a consciousness of balance. If I need help, I will ask for it and not be ashamed to seek assistance. With my adult self and child self in balance, I know that I can succeed.

I choose to live in the present.

I will live today in the present, rejoicing in each precious moment. For far too long I have lived in the pain and shame of the past or in fear about the future. I have spent most of my life inside my head, cut off from the rich experiences of the present moment.

Today I will not deny or repress the pain from my childhood but I won't get stuck there either. I will comfort the hurt child within me and seek to leave behind the bitterness that is robbing me of my life.

Today I will also resist the temptation to live in my elaborate plans and worries about the future. I will relieve my inner child of the need to anticipate the future in order to avoid danger. I was unable to relax and enjoy my childhood but I will not miss what life offers me in my adulthood.

Today I will embrace with joy all that this day has to give.

I have the courage to reach out to life.

The Cowardly Lion wanted courage. His fears immobilized him, keeping him from enjoying the kind of life he truly wanted. After facing his fears and acting in spite of them, he learned the true meaning of courage.

How many times can a toddler have her hand slapped before she stops reaching out to the world? Because I didn't get the kind of parenting I needed when I was a toddler, I have difficulty deciding what I want as an adult. When I am indecisive, I often feel discouraged.

The kind of life the deepest part of me desires is within my reach. Choosing the direction of my life takes courage. I need to be willing to act upon my decisions.

Today I will search within for the strength to redirect my life. Like the Cowardly Lion, I realize that the courage I long for is within me.

I seek balance in relationships.

I seek balance in my relationships. I receive friendship and love and I give friendship and love. I no longer rush into relationships, needy and demanding, seeking more than I could possibly hold or anyone could possibly give me. I can take care of my inner child who for so long was neglected and deprived of love.

I no longer feel the need to cling to a relationship for dear life. I will not turn myself inside out just to have someone, anyone in my life. I will not cease to be if I let go.

Today I will be cautious but confident in my choice of friends and intimate partners. In my recovery from co-dependency, I will trust the wisdom of my heart to guide me in the right direction, toward a balanced and harmonious relationship of give-and-take.

I transform envy into self-awareness.

Today I will accept envy as a valuable clue to uncovering my needs. I am confident in my ability to fulfill my desires.

Sibling rivalry is a fact of life. A younger child may envy an older sibling's achievements or abilities. An older child may envy the attention a newborn receives. In a healthy family, parents acknowledge that all children deserve nurturing and are capable of achievement. A wise mother or father looks beyond the envy and helps the child identify the underlying need.

My inner child did not receive help in working through the powerful experience of sibling rivalry. As an adult in recovery, I now allow myself to feel envy without guilt or shame. I transform my envy into a heightened awareness of my needs and wants. I am choosing positive actions that nurture my growth.

I will begin to live my life with a new peace.

Last night my heart was pounding, my mind racing. I was exhausted but I couldn't seem to relax. I awoke full of nervous tension, my mind on full alert. Scenarios of danger and catastrophe run in an unending loop through my weary brain.

I know I must free myself from the "fight or flight" cycle. I have been locked in its grip since childhood. The danger was very real then but it is not always real now. I know that if I do not train my body and my mind to relax, I will soon burn out.

Tonight I will break the cycle by choosing to release my tension. I will name my fears and worries, especially those over which I have no control and visualize myself offering them to my Higher Power.

As my Higher Power takes them from me, a sensation of well-being warms every inch of my body. Tonight I will begin to live my life with a new peace.

I am ready to go out into the world.

My inner child is strong and self-confident, in touch with her own thoughts and feelings. She can think for herself and make her own decisions. I am proud of her abilities and so is she. She is ready to go out into the world and I am ready to let her go.

Today I will give her a big hug and a kiss and watch as she sets out on her journey through life. I feel good because I know she will always come to me for comfort and advice. She feels good because she knows I am always here for her whenever she needs rest, encouragement, a hug. We love each other unconditionally.

I remember my inner child while I parent.

Today I will meet the needs of my children by nurturing my inner child.

At best, parenting is hard work. Sometimes I feel torn between the needs of my family and the needs of my inner child. My experience as a child left me with distorted attitudes that burden my parenting.

In my dysfunctional family, there was not enough love or time or energy for my needs to be met. Because of their own unresolved neediness, my parents expected me to take care of them. So I learned to deny my needs to please my parents. As a result, I, too, have many unresolved needs.

As an adult child in recovery, I am learning healthy living skills. By accepting responsibility for my own needs, I am better able to meet my children's needs. By my own example, I can teach my children what they need to know about living a healthy, happy life.

I open my eyes to all my choices today.

My knowledge of myself comes from a history of knowing what I like and don't like. My preferences in work come from experimenting with different jobs. My preferences in play result from having bad experiences as well as good. My preferences in relationships come from being open to many different types of people.

Healthy children play make-believe games and try on new behaviors. It is through play that children find out who they are.

In my alcoholic family, I had to grow up too soon; playing games was not tolerated. As an adult, I still struggle with who I am and what I really want. It is not too late to find myself.

The process of knowing myself is lifelong and opening my eyes to all my choices and experiences will help me to know myself better. Knowing myself, I will make better choices in the future.

Today I will say goodbye to defiance.

As a teenager, I developed the habit of saying no to my parents, to my teachers, to anyone who smacked of the status quo. I thought my belligerence proved what an independent thinker I was. I was proud of myself for making my own valiant way in the world, no matter how difficult.

Over the years my automatic nay-saying has exacted a heavy price. Unwilling to accept constructive criticism and well-intended suggestions, I have damaged my career and my relationships. Colleagues and friends keep their distance. My fear of giving in has left me on the outside, cold and lonely.

I no longer want to be the lonely hero fighting the whole world. Today I will invite others to share their ideas and desires with me. I will listen and respond with respect. I will rejoice in having valiant companions on my journey.

I will face my emptiness today.

Being alone has always been scary. What if I don't like who I am? What if my loneliness overwhelms me and I fall flat on my face? Now I realize that there is no way to avoid my feeling of aloneness. I may have tried relationships, sex or business to avoid the terror. All these behaviors leave me depleted, shameful and even emptier. Today I will choose to spend some time alone. I desire to learn how to be *with* myself.

I will quiet the inner voice that warns me of my emptiness. This voice is my scared inner child that was abandoned long ago. I will comfort this child with reassuring words, "I will be with you — I will never abandon you again."

Today I will begin to face my dark emptiness carrying a bright torch of courage and faith. My partner on this journey is my Higher Power, who is with me each step of the way.

Today is my re-birth day.

I have never understood the phrase "act your age." Perhaps it is because I surrendered my childhood very early. Being six years old and emotionally responsible for needy parents was necessary in my family. I had to put childish things aside to survive.

Now I am an adult with many responsibilities. I am serious, hard working, *very* responsible — yet, life feels so empty. Out of necessity, I choked the life out of my inner child long ago.

Today I will breathe life into my inner child, knowing it is never too late. I will begin by taking time to talk to him. How is my child feeling? What does my inner child need? Maybe he needs to play or to express himself. Mainly, he just needs me to love and care for him.

This is the day that I give birth to that precious inner child. I will mark this day as my re-birth day.

My physical needs are important.

Growing up in an alcoholic environment, I invested so much emotional energy in taking care of others that I neglected my own physical needs. Taking care of my body was not as important as helping someone else cope. Since no one was there to take care of me, I did not learn to take good care of myself.

Today is evaluation day. I will assess my physical needs remembering it is not selfish to take care of myself. Do I eat well-balanced nutritious meals? Do I drink enough water? Do I exercise regularly and vigorously? Do I get enough sleep? Do I take time for medical and dental check-ups? I will be honest with my answers.

Today I will do those things that are respectful to my body, my physical self.

Today I will gently push my limits.

Today I will flex my muscles and gently push my limits just a tiny bit further than yesterday. I will accept that some pain is normal for growth and welcome it. At the same time, I will be alert to damaging pain and stop pushing.

As a child, I never learned to work through difficult situations. I stopped playing piano when there were too many sharps and flats, I stopped doing math when I couldn't understand equations, I stopped trying to ride my bike up the big hill when my legs started to hurt. "If it's too hard, then quit," was my motto.

These days, I no longer am afraid of the pain that goes along with progress and change. I welcome it and know I will work through the pain to the next level of growth.

I will define and celebrate my own success.

Growing up in a dysfunctional family, I never learned how to set and achieve reasonable goals. I felt that I could never do enough. Regardless of how well I did, I could not celebrate my success.

In my recovery, I now measure my success in small increments. As I acknowledge each positive action I take to achieve my goal, I learn to organize my work in manageable steps. Relaxed and confident in my progress, I enjoy the process without worrying about the outcome.

Today I will praise each positive action I take toward achieving my goals. I will define and celebrate my own success.

Today I will follow my desires
and value my interests.

I may have grown up in a family that listened only to classical music and thought the Beatles were a passing fad, the sooner passed the better. Or my parents may have read only the sports page and *Dear Abby* in the newspaper and thought I was uppity if I read a history book. Something was wrong with my tastes and preferences. I was wasting my time stretching too far or stooping too low.

Today I can read what I desire — a romance novel or a scientific journal or both. I can listen to opera or country music or both. I can play tennis, do needlepoint or sit and stare out the window. Today I value my interests because they are a true reflection of who I am now.

Tomorrow I may change my tastes; I may explore new interests or rediscover old fancies. Today I will follow my desires, whatever they may be.

I can conquer my fear of letting others close.

I discovered as a child that my parents were not to be trusted. The very people who should have been the safest in my life were abusive and manipulative. In my dysfunctional family, keeping others distant was essential to my survival, so I walled myself off.

Now the walls that once protected me have become an impregnable fortress, shutting out the very people I care the most about. At times, I throw up walls of anger to drive others away. At other times, I withdraw into a black cloud of depression as a way to keep others out. Yet a part of me is empty and aches for emotional and physical closeness.

Today I will begin to bring down the walls of my fortress and seek to let others be close in appropriate ways. I will reassure the child within me that he can begin to relax, for I will love and take care of him even as I allow others to love and care for me.

I am making order out of chaos.

I honor the art of living freely. Each day becomes a work of art that I create with spontaneity, flexibility and structure.

Creating structure in my life is important. I need a solid foundation from which to grow. My addictive family did not provide me with the consistent structure that helped me feel safe in this world. Rules kept changing, promises were broken and there was nothing to depend on. Unless there is some order or structure in my life, I will not feel safe or secure. A child cannot feel free or spontaneous on a jungle gym that's broken.

Today I will comfort my inner child by making life manageable. If I need structure in my life, I will ask advice from a trusted friend or a sponsor. Perhaps I will attend 12-Step meetings, a therapy group or participate in a program of study or exercise. I am committed to making order out of chaos in my life.

**Today I will remain true to myself
and to my feelings.**

I remain true to myself and to my feelings. I act
ethically because it is the only response that
reflects my true self.

My recovery is an ethical response to the injustice of growing up in a dysfunctional family. I
do not have to blame my parents for their
imperfections and problems, but I recognize
that their failure to nurture and guide me was a
form of injustice.

As an adult, I take responsibility to restore justice for my inner child. I stand firm in asserting
rights for myself and others.

My ethics come not from a sense of duty but
from my sense of self. Once I have recovered
my authentic self, I will not surrender it.

Today I will remain true to myself and to my
feelings.

**I am protecting myself
with healthy boundaries.**

The small child pushes and pushes against the barrier, trying to move it. He backs up and runs, plowing into it. It remains where it is. After a few more attempts, he starts to play with something else, satisfied the barrier will not change. His play area is something he can count on.

In my dysfunctional family, the boundaries changed all the time. Sometimes I would go to where the boundaries had been — only to discover they were gone. As a result, limits and boundaries are things I didn't know were mine to have.

In recovery, I am learning it is okay for me to set up boundaries around myself. I can choose them and enforce their limits. This means that I can leave a situation if someone is abusive or even say no when I disagree. Today I will allow myself to begin enforcing boundaries that will make my environment safe and dependable.

I nurture my infant self with love.

I respect my infant self as a person. I respect his vulnerability. I protect him and at the same time I begin to let him go so that he can develop his own strengths. He is like no other infant. I respect and marvel at his uniqueness.

I gaze into his eyes and he gazes into mine. In this way, we nurture each other with love. I listen for and to his cries because they are his only means of communication. Then I gladly give him the food, warmth, embrace or freedom he needs when he needs it.

Together we begin a new life.

I will forgive by letting go of judgments.

Today I choose to forgive all those who have hurt me, not for their sake but for mine. I have sought to forgive my offenders before but my bitterness continues to surface like waste rising from the bottom of a polluted lake. It's time to cleanse the poisons that have polluted my life. I know the offenders from my past will continue to live as uninvited guests within my memory unless I can release my resentment, with their hurtful roles in my life. Each replay of old scenes keeps my wounds raw and unhealed.

Today I will truly forgive my past foes by letting go of my need to judge. Today I will visualize myself releasing those who have hurt me, out of my court of judgment into God's court of judgment. After all, God is better able to dispense justice than I am. My spirit lightens as the emotional baggage that I have carried for so long falls away. In releasing those I have held prisoner, I see now that I was the real prisoner.

I will recognize my fear of abandonment.

As a child, my parents abandoned me emotionally. They were cold and moody and self-absorbed. Only on rare occasions did they act loving and then only with strings attached.

In my adult relationships, I still feel the same fear in the pit of my stomach. The child within me still cringes at the possibility of emotional abandonment. A word, a tone of voice or gesture — or lack of it — can drive me to act in ways that I think will prevent a friend or lover from leaving me. Yet my dishonest behavior only serves to reinforce the message of shame that says I will never be acceptable to another as I am. In the end my role-playing and people-pleasing are just attempts to control others and keep them from leaving me.

Today I will not acquiesce to my fear of abandonment. I will be myself with confidence, knowing how much I have to bring to any relationship.

Today I will make healthy decisions.

As a child, I was controlled by events around me. I had no choice but to put up with haphazard schedules, broken promises and undependability. As an adult, my attempts to make choices turn into a three-ring circus and I feel confused.

The things I've learned in recovery will come to my aid now. The concepts can help me to look with a rational mind at confusing events and evaluate them. When the choices of others conflict with mine, I don't have to become overwhelmed. My adult self can calm my frenzied child inside.

I can make new choices. I can still achieve some of my goals even though others are thwarted. Events no longer control my life. Nor do I control my life with a tight fist. I know that when I let go, I continue to grow.

I let myself get as much sleep as I need.

Growing is hard work. It's hard on the body, the mind and the emotions. Sometimes I feel like I need to sleep for a week just to catch up but so much needs to be done. So I drink coffee to keep awake and keep going. I'm exhausted!

As a loving and responsible parent, I know that my inner child needs plenty of rest each day to grow and develop. So I make sure that he gets to bed on time and that his bed is a place of comfort and renewal. I tell him it's okay to get as much sleep as he needs. I help him crawl into bed and wrap himself up warmly in the covers. I hold him as he drifts off to sleep. He sleeps until his body signals it's time to wake and he wakes refreshed and ready to start a new day.

I can calm my own fears.

Sometimes the child within me sits straight up in the dark, terrified, unable to sleep. Every noise is frightening. Worries that seem overwhelming fill the air. When this happens, I know what to do.

First I make sure she's surrounded by soft warmth — perhaps some stuffed animals or a big pillow she can hug. Then I soothe her body with warm milk or hot chocolate. When she settles down, we can talk. "I know something is bothering you," I say, "and it's important enough to keep you up at night. But we can talk it over in the morning, see what's wrong and work on ways to solve the problem. Right now it's important to get to sleep and be well rested for the day ahead. This is your special time to relax."

Together we lie down, snuggle in the pillows and blankets, close our eyes and drift off to sleep.

I accept the transitions in my life.

Today I will let go of my obsessive need to resolve immediately all that is unresolved in my life. I will be patient and trust that the outcome, whatever it is, will be in my best interest. I survived in my dysfunctional family by being able to anticipate danger and take steps to avoid it. Now, as an adult, I become anxious and worried when I can't predict the outcome of a situation.

Yet life is not always painted in black and white. Many issues fall inside the gray zone, where issues cannot be immediately resolved and loose ends dangle in an untidy mess. I know that the next step I must take along my path toward personal growth involves learning to live in the gray zone.

I will give up my demand that all my life situations be quickly resolved. Even when I cannot predict the outcome of a situation, I will trust that all will be well. Today I will be comfortable living with transitions.

My thoughts and feelings are my own.

My thoughts and feelings belong to me. No one else can tell me what I *really* think, when I *really* feel. I don't have to check with others to see what they're feeling and thinking so that I'll know what I "should" feel or think.

As a child, I was often told that my feelings about this or that situation were wrong. I shouldn't be angry that my sister got a present and I didn't; I should be happy it was her birthday. I shouldn't hate Uncle Jim; I should love him because he's my uncle. My faith in the validity of my own mind was undermined early on.

Now I am an adult. I know that I have the right to own my thoughts and feelings. They may be good, bad, mean, spiteful, helpful, hurtful, wonderful, indifferent. Whatever they are, they belong to me.

I am taking full responsibility for my life.

A schooner sails the heavy seas, slicing through the swells. The captain mans the wheel, holding fast to the wooden spokes. One of his men calls directions, but mostly he sails by intuition.

As a child, I felt like I was on a ship battered by a stormy raging sea because my parents, the captains of the family, abandoned their posts. As a recovering adult, my life is still a voyage—one of discovery. I am discovering the core issues that prevent me from enjoying life and the specific fears that inhibit the achievement of my full potential. I am discovering my motivations so that I can make clear decisions about life, directing my own schooner on a safe voyage. It is a comfort to my inner child that I am becoming an expert navigator. All of my discoveries help me to take full responsibility for my life.

Just like the captain who will not leave his post when his schooner hits rough seas, I will not abandon myself when the seas of life threaten to overwhelm me.

I am in touch with my spirituality.

As a child, religion was not a refuge; it was a trap from which I wanted to escape. Sitting through religious services made me feel claustrophobic. I felt oppressed, not uplifted. My parents called themselves religious but their behavior was abusive and shaming. Religion seemed to have nothing to do with me or my life. I wanted nothing to do with it.

I feel a need now to touch my spiritual center. My spirituality exists apart from the organized religion of my childhood, yet I can use it to support and reinvigorate my religious foundation if I choose. I envision my spirituality as a well deep within me. I can dip into this well as many times as I need to for it never will run dry. Its waters refresh and soothe me.

Today I will drink joyfully from this infinite well of love.

I can let go.

At this moment I will let go of all the hurts and pains I have been holding on to since child-hood. This burden of woe weighs too heavily, taxing the strength and energy I need to change and grow.

Today I will drop my burden. I am amazed by how light I feel. I automatically stand up straight-er and see much further than I could before. Freed from holding on, my hands can explore new possibilities. I revel in my newfound free-dom of movement. Letting go, my hands are free to grab on to life.

I applaud my bravery.

My inner child is brave and daring. I am the hero (or the heroine) of epic adventures while my recovery guides me along new paths to new lands.

As a young child, I delighted in fairy tales of brave men and women battling dragons and outsmarting evil wizards. As I grew older, I sought role models in sports, the arts, science and religion.

I may have imagined myself accepting accolades as a brilliant scientist, a fearless explorer, a gifted musician. My inner child lived each fantasy as a story that could come true.

In recovery, I have lived the fantasies of my inner child. I have battled the dragons of co-dependency and the ghosts of despair. I have reaped the rewards of exciting discoveries and healthy living. Today I will applaud my bravery and daring and I will fearlessly seek adventure in my recovery.

**I belong to nature and I live within
the order of nature.**

Children begin learning about differences at
an early age and one of their first teachers is
nature. Children find their place in the natural
order through comparisons. They learn that
they have power over their actions and they do
not have power over other people, the sun and
stars or God. My inner child needs information
to begin to make distinctions. In my dysfunctional family, I did not learn facts about my
body and facts about the natural world. Nature
reproduces, but sex was a shameful secret in
my family. All living beings die, but someone's
death was an overwhelming and unresolved
experience for my parents.

Today I observe the world about me. I watch
leaves in the sunlight. Perhaps I will find a
book about the part of nature I am most
interested in. Today I will acknowledge that I
belong to the world and I am part of nature.

I give myself and my inner
child time to grow.

A bird begins its journey into life as an embryo safe inside its shell. There, in the darkness, it has all the nourishment, warmth and protection it needs to develop. From the outside, it seems as though nothing is happening. Yet if left alone until the right time, the chick confidently pecks away the outer shell and emerges into the light ready for life.

Like a bird, I too need time to develop. I too can draw a protective shell of warmth and nourishment around me, feeding my needs, taking all the time I need. It may not look to others as if much is happening and I too may be impatient. Nevertheless, I will pay attention to the quiet wisdom of my inner voice. Then, when I know I'm ready, I will confidently crack my shell and be born into the light.

Today my inner child bubbles.

Bubble bath . . . bubblegum . . . toy bubbles . . . carbonated bubbles. Today even my inner child bubbles.

Feelings are not always heavy and intense. As an adult in recovery, I am learning a wide range of feelings. Happiness may be powerfully exuberant or softly joyful. Happiness may be as light and frivolous as a bubble.

During my childhood, heaviness hovered over my family like a permanent dark cloud. No one claimed the feeling or connected it to any event. I experienced feelings as vague and general and I thought they would last forever.

Today I will delight in delicate sensations. Rainbow colors shimmer. Fizzies tickle my nose. Transparent balls rise and float above the ground. Feeling light and airy, I will rise above my fears and worries.

I can communicate clearly.

I have a three-year-old within who never learned to use words because no one ever seemed to listen to them. He had to get what he wanted by whining or crying or grunting until someone finally paid attention. I'm hurt now when others misinterpret my intentions or get angry at me for becoming upset and frustrated.

When I feel misunderstood, I will not become paralyzed by my own frustration. Instead, I will pause and communicate with my three-year-old. I will speak slowly and reassure him with clear language that he can understand. He doesn't have to whine or cry or grunt to get my attention. Today I will listen to my three-year-old and delight in watching him become a thinking person.

I will be the initiator today.

Do you see the little child hanging back, behind the tree? It's me. I'm afraid to come out, afraid to play ball, afraid to start anything at all.

"Don't initiate anything!" the warning voices fly. "You might get hurt. You might be rejected." And so I no longer want to try.

Today is the day to change all that. Today is the day I can initiate anything I want. I can ask for what my inner child wants. I can be the one to begin. It feels good to begin. My soul radiates new energy and light.

Today I will not be afraid to initiate something I've wanted to try for a long time. I no longer need to hide behind the tree.

Today I will let go of my need to judge.

In my dysfunctional family, I needed to be right. It was my way of protecting myself from unfair and needless accusations. Being judgmental was a good offense. It kept my own feelings of inadequacy and self-loathing hidden from me.

As a child, I couldn't have survived those feelings. Now I know that when I judge others, it's like throwing blankets over their heads. All I see is my own blanket, I never see who is standing in front of me. My judgment does nothing but make them "wrong" so that I can be "right."

Today I will let go of the need to judge others. I no longer need others to be wrong just to build my own self-worth. I will loosen my rigid perceptions of people, knowing that they have the right to be who they are. Like me, they are doing the best they can.

Today I resign from the blame game.

Today I am officially resigning as a participant in the blame game. It is a game I have played all my life and it has become an obsession.

The blame game was a favorite pastime in my addicted family. Mistakes were immediately followed by emotional exchanges over who was at fault. I often was blamed, and I learned to blame others just as readily. In my adult life, the blame game has become an obsession. Sometimes I blame others and then am consumed with anger and bitterness. Or I take the blame and am swept up in a cycle of guilt and shame. Both responses divert energy from solving the problem and getting on with life.

Today if my inner child reacts out of hurt and fear, I will gently take control and thrust thoughts of blame out of my mind. I will replace them with thoughts of peace and tolerance, thereby rescuing both myself and others from the destruction wrought by the blame game.

I can play with my inner child.

Today I will rejoice in my ability to play with my inner child. My inner child loves to play and needs to play. His play is his work, the way he learns how to live in the world. We enjoy playing together — exploring, discovering, experimenting, having fun. I use my imagination but I don't dictate the rules. I allow him to create the game. I let my inner child lead me into play.

When I was a child, someone was always telling me when to play, what to play, how to play. The games I liked were always bad or wrong or silly. Someone was always trying to show me a better way. It was so frustrating! I never experienced the freedom of what it's like to have fun.

Today I will embrace the healing power of play as I energize myself and the child within. I will remember that when I honor my inner child, I am in touch with the qualities of spontaneity, flexibility and joy.

It's okay to be on my own.

Today I understand that it's okay to be on my own. I am comfortable with myself and I'm a good companion. I no longer worry about being smart enough or good enough or powerful enough to manage in the world. I am all of these and more.

It was difficult for me to leave home. I never had the support for growing up. My parents always seemed to undermine my need for independence: "Are you sure you know what you're doing? You'll never make it out there all alone." So even though I finally did leave, I felt scared and vulnerable and incapable of taking care of myself.

Today I will tell my inner child, "It's time. I'm proud of you for wanting to go out and be on your own. You have the skills you need to survive and friends you can call on for support. And you know I'll always be here for you."

I am centered in stability and contentment.

Today I will take my growth toward health another step forward. I will tend to my emotional needs instead of focusing on the needs of others.

As a child, I was taught that my emotional needs didn't matter. I grew up without a clear sense of what made me happy or unhappy. In recovery, I have learned to protect myself from the negative emotions of others. No longer am I a receptacle for others' unhappiness. Now I must also learn to tend and cultivate my own inner emotional life.

Today, regardless of the people or the circumstances around me, I will keep guard over the delicate inner design of my emotions. When threatened by attacks from without or critical voices from within, I will notice them and restore them to peace with positive affirmations. I will create a center within me today of emotional stability.

Today I will open myself to warmth and joy.

The summer sun warms the grass while birds
dart and soar overhead. Wrapped in a light
blanket, a baby absorbs the sun's rays with a
hint of a grin on his face. The rays caress and
soothe like a mother's gentle hand. The sun
nurtures him.

When I was a baby, my parents had little time or
energy to nurture me. I instinctively felt devoid
of something special and essential. Instead of
focusing on what my parents did not or could
not do, I can heal those empty places myself by
nurturing the needy infant within me. The sun
can nurture me today if I set aside some time to
be outdoors. Any activity will do: working in
the garden, taking a long walk, lying still on a
blanket, riding my bike or playing golf. I will
take notice of the sun's warmth against my skin.
My body relaxes as the rays melt away tension.
With little effort, I can allow nature to fill me.
The infant inside of me feels cared for as I open
myself to warmth and joy.

I still have needs and it's okay!

A cry of need bursts forth from the lungs of an infant without shame. "My tummy hurts!" she screams with a lusty cry. "Please fill it with something warm and soothing."

"Just hold me," a little boy calls out in wordless tears. "Touch me, rock me, be close."

Even as adults, our deepest needs cry out. We, too, need to be filled, touched, loved and rocked. Our inner child calls to those around us to take care of us and satisfy our needs for nurturing. In shame, I have hidden my needs and refused to cry out.

Today I will care for them. I may bask in the warmth of a bubble bath, seek a hug from a friend or brew a special cup of tea while surrounded and rocked with gentle music.

I am in charge of my world.

When I was a child, I had no power. When I spoke, no one heard me. My voice was too weak and tentative to have an effect. Even though I'm an adult now, I still feel powerless to affect change at times.

I wasn't in charge of my world when I was a child but I can take charge of my inner world now. Using the power of my imagination, I can return to my childhood and heal the wounds that still fester.

In my mind, I can take the hand of my inner child and explore past hurts. I stand by my inner child, providing strong support. When someone hurts my child, I speak up with conviction. I can see situations clearly now. I take charge of myself and my child as I make peace with my own personal history.

Today I have the power to affect change within myself. This is what recovery is all about.

My story gives meaning to my survival.

I am the storyteller because I have survived. In recovery, I tell the story of my past from the viewpoint of a survivor, not a victim.

In families, stories are handed down to connect the generations. We rely on the stories to tell us about our family and what we were like as babies. In dysfunctional families, these stories may be distorted or untold to protect the family secrets. Because this happened in my family, I could only guess at what was true.

In recovery I tell my story to people I trust, and in the telling, I create the meaning of my life. I listen to other survivors and together we create connections that bind us together as survivors. My story gives meaning to my survival.

I take pride in my body.

At the beach I see children of all ages. A toddler scoops sand into a bucket; an eight-year-old leaps and hits the water with a splash.

Then I watch groups of teenaged girls and boys strut back and forth along the shore, each body announcing "I am a woman" or "I am a man." They move as if wearing new clothes — careful not to cause a single wrinkle, a little uncertain but undeniably proud.

As a teenager, I had mixed feelings about my body as it matured. One day I wanted to be sexy and sophisticated. Another day I wanted to forget my body and play like an eight-year-old. I confused physical maturity with sexual maturity. I felt burdened by my gender.

Today I own both my body and my sexuality. I can distinguish between my need for physical touch and my need for sexual expression. I take pride in my body and I meet my physical and sexual needs responsibly.

I create a healthy home for my children.

My childhood was filled with secrets. Doors closed as I walked by. Conversations stopped in mid-sentence when I came into the room. I was certain everyone was talking about me. I was positive that something must be terribly wrong with me. My shame became my secret.

Today I will have no more secrets. In my mind's eye, I will open all the doors and windows in my childhood house and let in fresh air.

With no closed doors to hide behind, the voices from the past ring clear. They are not talking about me, they are only concerned with themselves and their problems. Finally, I can release the shame that has for so long infected my life. My parents' problems belong to them, not to me.

Cleansed, I can create a healthy home where secrets don't exist. In this environment, my children and I will flourish.

I integrate my roles into one identity.

There are many roles that I play. In the course of one day I may be a worker, a friend or a lover.

In my recovery, I've learned the appropriate time and place for these roles. I integrate all my roles into one identity, and I am open to exploring new ones.

Appropriate behavior and timing were not something I learned from my family. Taking care of parents whose behavior was inappropriate, limited my opportunities. The rigidity of my family prevented me from trying on new ways of being. The chaos did not provide me with the structure needed for developing my identity.

Today my emerging sense of self gives me the foundation for flexible and comfortable interactions with others. My inner child delights as I explore the richness of who I am.

I embrace the totality of my being.

As I recover, I affirm my right to become a whole person — emotionally, spiritually, mentally and physically. I embrace the totality of my being, thereby affirming my inner child.

My task is to fulfill the potential of my whole being. I cannot accomplish this by breaking myself into parts.

My whole being grows when any part of me grows. When I express my feelings, I express my spirituality. When my spirituality deepens, my whole self reflects its impact. My clear thinking affects all of me, and caring for my body nurtures my mind and spirit.

My inner child is grounded in the knowledge of my wholeness. Today I will rest assured that my recovery embodies my totality.

I celebrate my independence as the splendor of a fireworks display.

Today I announce my independence with the forcefulness of whistling flares. I am strong, I am competent, I am free. My positive messages shake the skies and prepare the way for new displays of growth.

My goals soar as high as the shooting sky-rockets. As I separate my values and choices from those of my parents, I am removing limits to my freedom. I am farther and higher than ever before and my dreams light up the sky. My skills and talents unfold as a Roman candle and my achievements explode in a canopy of sizzling color. I hear the oohs and ahs of the audience and I acknowledge the well-deserved applause.

Today I celebrate my independence by brightening the sky with fireworks of positive messages, soaring dreams and splendid achievements.

Today I will protect my feelings with healthy reflexes.

Reflexes protect the body. A sneeze helps to blow dust and other irritants out of the nose. Shivers warm the body with quick muscle movements. Reflexes are outside the realm of conscious control.

In recovery, I am developing emotional reflexes that protect me. I am aware of put-downs that people make in conversations. I sense my discomfort and then I act. I may change the subject or end the conversation.

I pay attention to "crazy" feelings when my mind blanks out around certain family members. I no longer participate in the unhealthy behaviors that I learned in my dysfunctional family.

Today I will protect my feelings with healthy reflexes and restore my inner harmony with positive actions.

I can tell the whole story.

Today I will give my inner child permission to tell her whole story. She need not hold anything back. She can voice her anger without fear of hurting anyone or being hurt by them.

My family never told anyone the whole story. We only heard the parts we were allowed to hear. So I became adept at piecing together information and reading tones of voice. Often, I could discern the truth on the basis of what *wasn't* being said rather than on what was said.

My parents claimed they were protecting me. They made excuses. It was for my own good. It was none of my business. Their secrecy and dishonesty made me feel angry and powerless.

Today I will practice discernment and openness. If I am talking to someone I trust, I can speak openly and share my feelings and thoughts. If I am with strangers, I will protect myself and share what feels safe.

I let my sensual inner child direct me.

Inside of me lives a child who never had a chance to crawl and toddle her way around to explore her world. Too many rules and too many restrictions kept her on a tight rein. She aches to be able to roam freely, making discoveries for herself. Today I will free my inner toddler to explore her world.

Here is a book. I know a book is for reading, but my toddler doesn't. She drops it on the floor. Thud! Oh, it's heavy! What's this? I can open it. Oh, it smells musty. The whooshing sound as my fingers rifle through the pages intrigue her.

I will make the world safe for my toddler's explorations. I will allow her to make her own judgments, to learn about her world on her own terms, at her own speed. When I allow myself to explore, I learn to fill the gaping holes of my sabotaged childhood. Today I take the world in through my senses and I let my sensual inner child direct me.

I strengthen my reality when
I trust my perceptions.

My inner child is attuned to contradiction. When someone's words and feelings do not match, the child within notes the discrepancy. My dysfunctional family was full of such discrepancies and in time I learned to mistrust my perceptions.

As an adult, my mistrust of my sense of reality sometimes means that I do not question unreasonable demands at work or within relationships. "I care about you but I'm too busy to listen," is a contradiction if my friend rarely lets me share my feelings. In recovery, I pay attention to the confused feelings produced by such contradictions. I let my inner child note the discrepancy and I choose the best course of action. I may ask questions, set clear limits or end a relationship.

Today I will trust my perceptions to guide my actions.

My inner child guides my focus.

When the huge world of possibilities over-whelms me, my inner child guides my focus. I remember how children concentrate upon mi-nute detail and immerse themselves in one object. They block out noise and distraction and hear only an inner voice.

When they are done, they return to the bustling world refreshed and ready for new adventures. My inner child is wise and intuitively knows that the smallest detail or simplest object adds a possibility for my growing sense of self.

Today I follow my inner child's urging. I focus my senses on one object or detail, a color, a brick wall or a potted flower. I do not force my attention or understanding. I observe with re-laxed concentration.

My inner child guides me to a new experience and a new self.

I can make new choices and experience new things.

Today I will begin to let go of the past. As a child in a dysfunctional family, I had to get used to constant change and chaos. Never knowing what situation I would encounter, I would come home from school with tremendous anxiety. So I attempted to control situations and people as much as possible. Clutching onto the familiar brought security and safety. Reaching out for the new and unfamiliar brought too much fear.

Today I will let go of the familiar and experience something new. I will eat at a new restaurant, play tennis with a new friend, experiment with a new recipe or simply take a new route home.

Today I will gradually begin to let go of the past. I will broaden my choices and take new risks.

I can let down my defenses.

When I was a child, I felt vulnerable and unprotected. For me life was frightening and I could be attacked without warning or reason at any time.

Block by block I built a fort of ice and snow around me so that no one could harm me. I grew up in there, protected from hurt but cut off from warmth. As an adult, I remained trapped in a child's snow fort, cold and isolated, defending myself from an enemy who no longer exists. Now in recovery, I know I don't need this shelter anymore. I can take care of myself.

Today I will let down my defenses. I can let my walls slowly grow smaller and smaller until they disappear and I am left standing in the warmth of the first day of spring. The sun's healing light begins to work its magic and I step with confidence into the new day.

I can relax without guilt.

Sometimes I feel out of control, driven relentlessly by an unending cycle of activity. When this happens, I sense a desperate little girl running from room to room trying to find someone to hold her.

Yet whenever I want to slow down and take it easy, critical voices from my childhood lash out, "Lazy, good-for-nothing!" I know that when I let myself be driven by these inner voices, I am still trying to please an unseen audience from my past.

Tonight I will relax without guilt. I will lie back in my most comfortable chair and enjoy my favorite music or daydream in front of a cozy fire. Tomorrow I will sit in the sun and do nothing, letting all my tensions evaporate. I will begin to take one day at a time as an important step toward taking care of myself.

I live my life as a sexual being.

My sexuality is my life force. It is the magnificent expression of my humanness. I participate in all of life as a sexual being. My sexuality is distinct — but it is connected to my spirituality, my feelings, my actions and my thoughts. I express my "aliveness" and my uniqueness through my sexuality.

As an adult child, I have felt guilty in expressing my uniqueness in any way. The loyalty demands of a dysfunctional family permit few differences and prevent healthy separation and detachment. I fulfilled other family members' sexual needs by denying my own.

As an adult in recovery, I detach my desires from the desires of others and I choose to meet my sexual needs responsibly. Today I will affirm my uniqueness through my sexual expression.

I am satisfied with who I am.

Growing up in my co-dependent family, I never felt approved of, no matter how hard I worked or what my accomplishments were. As a result, I found little satisfaction in anything I did. Now in adult life, despite my success, I often experience that same free-floating dissatisfaction. Sometimes it manifests itself as a dark cloud of depression, even though everything is going well. At the heart of the gray fog of negative feelings within me, I see the child who never received the acceptance that would have freed him to truly enjoy the good thing he had accomplished.

Today I will nurture and encourage my inner child. I will reassure him that who he is is wonderful, that he has no need to prove his acceptability by striving for even higher levels of accomplishment. As I encourage him, I feel the stirrings of self-satisfaction in who I am and in what I have accomplished. Today enough is finally enough.

I will be gentle with the scared child within.

A child is crying. When I cannot bear the sobs, my inner child hides in a closet, under a tree or in the attic. But she is there, weeping for what is lost, what never was, what never can be.

My inner child hides, afraid to be hurt again, feeling safe only in her hiding place. Yet alone she will find no solace. She needs to be comforted, loved and reassured. "You are a wonderful person." "I will take care of you." "I'm so happy you are here, alive and growing."

Children who have been hurt are shy and afraid to trust. Trust comes with gentle, persistent patience. So I, too, will have gentle, persistent patience with the frightened child within me. I will encourage her to come out where I can hold her, nurture her and give her a reason to trust. Today I will care for myself by comforting my inner child.

I see myself through the eyes
of my inner child.

How silly it is to sit on chairs when the floor isn't half as crowded. Besides, you never fall off the floor. In fact, sitting is pretty silly when you can roll, run, jump or tumble.

Grown-ups are really silly on the telephone. Sometimes their voices change and they sound like the people who do commercials — unbelievably polite.

Another thing, adults say goodbye 40 times before they ever leave their friends' houses. I could play ten games of Parcheesi between the time they say clean up the mess and we finally walk out.

Today I will see my adult self through the eyes of my inner child.

My happiness comes from within
and I share it with others.

Entering into a relationship with the expectation that another person can make me happy and content is a setup for failure. As a child, I believed that I was responsible for the unhappiness of my parents. I thought I needed to live up to their idea of a model child. I spent my days searching for something I could do to make their lives better.

Today I will let go of my need for others to live up to my ideals. I do not have the right to impose my expectations on anyone else. Today I will start relieving others of the responsibility for making me happy. I deserve a relationship, not to make me happy but in order to share the richness of who I am with another.

As I learn to recognize and meet my own needs, I depend less on others to fill me up. As I nurture my inner child, I become freer to engage with another in a healthy way.

I like myself just because I'm me.

I like myself just because I'm me.

I am unique and that makes me special. No one else can claim my place in the world. I don't have to be "more like my sister" or "more like my brother." I don't have to live the life my parents envisioned for me. I'm smart enough, funny enough, happy enough, sad enough, strong enough and wise enough just the way I am.

I like myself just because I'm me.

I will celebrate the joy of being myself.

My self-image is a collage made up of an odd assortment of individuals. Everyone I've ever wanted to be lives there, along with everyone I've ever been afraid of being. Hero and bum, saint and sinner, all take their turns in dominating both how I see myself and how I act.

My inner child, who is the heart of my true self, is neither a hero nor a bum. Each extreme arises from shame. The hero drives me to be more than I really am to prove my acceptability and my worth. The bum is merely a twisted product of the critical voices from my childhood, not a true reflection of me at all.

Today I will take another step on my journey toward wholeness by erasing both the heroes and the bums from my self-image. I am a human being — nothing more, nothing less. Today I will celebrate the joy of being myself — unique, special and acceptable just as I am.

I am filled with spiritual riches
and live an abundant life.

I possess a wealth of wisdom to identify the needs of my inner child. I am richly endowed with courage to face my feelings and express them directly. Consequently, I do not substitute unconditional love for my inner child with expensive cars or stereo systems. I do not stuff my feelings inside a closet crammed with clothes or gadgets. My abundant inner power fills me with peace of mind.

In my dysfunctional family I was deprived of nurturing. As an adult child, I avoided feeling the pain of deprivation through addictive behaviors. I tried to fill my emptiness with things rather than heal myself from within.

Today I will give the child within me the gifts of inner riches. I am filled with healing energy and peace of mind. I am rich in spiritual resources and I live an abundant life.

I can be content even when I am alone.

I will be content today inside or outside a committed relationship. As I have progressed in my recovery, I have grown to like myself more and more. My contentment with myself has given me a new freedom to be alone without panic or depression.

At times my inner child has driven me to cling to relationships to fill the need for belonging, a need that was never met in my dysfunctional family. I have come to see that I must create a place of belonging within myself, before I can ever share a home with someone else.

As part of my growth, I have become the loving, responsible parent my inner child never had. I have also learned to take time for myself. I use this time to enjoy life and to be with many friends without clinging to any one exclusive relationship. Today I will be happy with myself and with the richness of the life I am creating, whether I am alone or with someone else.

I accept my inner child.

As a child, I envied children who could be who they were without frowns of disapproval from those around them. I envied their careless play, the silliness of their decisions and fullness of their emotions.

As an adult, my envy disappears as I learn to accept my inner child. I realize the importance of being who I am rather than being the person I think others want me to be.

When my inner child takes over, I find that it doesn't matter what others think of me. Many people like me just as I am, without facade or pretense. Those who don't, aren't worth my time.

Once I was afraid to show who I really was to new friends, because I was certain they would go away. Now I realize that it is no loss to be without people in my life who have expectations I cannot fulfill. I am who I am — and I am good enough.

I can communicate without yelling.

In my chaotic family, someone was always shouting. We didn't discuss things rationally or speak quietly. Whoever could yell the loudest was the one who got heard. Whoever could shout the other down, won. This is what I learned to call communication.

Today I will listen to my inner child. He does not shout to be heard or verbally bully others into submission. He expresses himself clearly and succinctly, even in anger. As I listen to him, he learns to listen to me. Together we begin to communicate.

I will grant myself a pardon
for past mistakes.

Today I will come down from the attic of my past. I have been living up there for too long, sorting through a chest of old rags, rags of guilt and shame. Critical voices from my childhood contributed most of the rags in the chest — voices that told me I was never good enough, that I must always do more or be more to be acceptable. The voices of shame from my childhood are the voices of my dysfunctional parents.

Today I will replace their voices with a new voice, that reminds me of all the wonderful qualities God has given me. I will soothe my pangs of guilt over past failures by pardoning myself for being less than perfect. In doing so, I will absolve my inner child.

Today I will come down from the attic of my past and shut the door firmly behind me. I no longer have to live in the past. The sunshine and joy of life are waiting for me.

I can express my anger in a healthy way.

Sometimes my anger overwhelms me. Because as I was growing up I saw too many scenes of rage and violence, I vowed never to show my anger to anyone.

Yet sometimes I feel as if I have a two-year-old inside who wants to kick and scream and bite and tear. I become scared of my own rage and helpless to comfort this child within.

From now on when I feel like tearing up the world, I will envision my rampaging two-year-old. I will gently embrace him to keep him from hurting himself, until his rage loses its power. I feel the rigidity leave his body. He allows sadness to wash over him and grows stronger as he is allowed to verbalize his anger.

As I learn to disarm my rage, I can be clearer and more direct with my anger. I can learn to express emotions in a healthy way.

I experience the flow between
my head and my heart.

As a two-year-old, I tried to assert independent thought and action. My will automatically pushed against my parents' will, demanding that boundaries be set. In my childhood home, such independence was not tolerated. Consequently, my thoughts and emotions whirl in great confusion in my adult life. Sometimes I become obsessed, letting my thoughts churn and churn, so I do not have to feel. At other times, my feelings become so intense that I am unable to think about them.

Today I will experience the delicate dance between my head and my heart. If sadness or pain overwhelms me, I will take time to ask what the emotion is telling me. In this way I will allow the wisdom of my emotions and the structure of my thoughts to balance. I will become the gentle and firm parent that my two-year-old needs.

I have every right to be here.

No thoughts enter my mind and I have trouble concentrating. It is okay for me to be still, to let nothingness take over where my thoughts usually play and direct. I will allow myself to relax and absorb the stimuli around me without shaming myself.

Today I will leave undone that which can be left undone for another day without berating myself for not doing it. I will not hurry from one task to another. I will allow myself as much time as I need.

Today I will take care of the wonderful infant inside me. Perhaps I will sit in the sunshine and let the breeze play with my hair. Or maybe I will stay in bed and doze. Or maybe I will take a leisurely walk and listen to the sounds of my world. I will simply *be*. And that's okay.

I am learning the art of being with others.

Healthy children learn to assert themselves when they need companionship. They can name their loneliness, walk into a room and enjoy the mere presence of other people around them.

The aloneness that I experienced growing up in my addicted family was often too much to bear. Sometimes I felt like a nuisance if I needed my parents' attention. Other times I had to entertain or perform to earn their presence. Feeling alone in a house full of people was devastating.

Today I will fulfill my desire to connect with others. If I am working alone or at home and want company, I may invite a friend or family member to join me. I am learning the art of being with others in comfortable silence instead of frenetic anxiety.

I am capable of finding companionship in my life. I meet this need simply and with confidence.

Today my child within and I
reach for the stars!

Sometimes I let opportunities pass. I'm afraid to take risks and try new things. The opportunity to make a new friend frightens me. What if he or she hurts me? The opportunity to advance in a new job only makes me aware of my inadequacies. Could I really move to a new town? Could I really do the work?

The opportunity to become emotionally healthy is equally as frightening. What if it hurts too much? What if I learn things I never really wanted to know? Yet my child within is bubbling over with energy today, daring me to exceed my limits and try new things.

Today I will seek new opportunities. I will take a risk and reach for the stars, remembering that courage comes from facing fear and going ahead anyway. I will make the most of every opportunity, discovering the energy that comes with action.

I enliven and enrich the world about me.

My perceptions of the world are grounded in reality and my actions are positive and powerful.

My inner child experiences the world through her senses, thoughts and feelings. She has personal power that makes me noticed when I walk into a room or makes people respond to my smiles and observations. My presence affects the world about me.

In my dysfunctional family, I felt that I had little or no impact on those around me, assuming that my presence caused only pain and suffering. In recovery, I acknowledge my inner child's personal power and perceptions. I move through the world with confidence.

Today I will choose actions that affirm and enrich my life and the lives of others.

I can give myself a break.

When I'm tired, I allow myself to rest. I stay in bed, wrapped up in the warm cozy blankets for as long as I wish. If I want to, I go back to sleep. When I get up, I move slowly, take a long hot bath or shower, and rub my body with oils or creams that make me feel smooth and pampered. I devote one whole day to taking care of myself.

Today I no longer am the child who had to get sick in order to slow down. I pay attention to my needs before I come down with a fever or a sore throat or a headache. Every so often I pamper myself by allowing myself to stay home from work. I watch TV or read a book, eat my favorite foods and just relax. I don't have to be sick anymore to take care of myself.

I respond rationally to authority.

In dysfunctional families, parents have little knowledge of how to help children grow. Their authority is often used irrationally and their children respond from fear.

As an adult child, I often respond to authority irrationally. Either I follow orders unquestioningly and work beyond reasonable limits on my job or I become defiant and rebel against all authority.

Through my recovery, I am learning to monitor my response to authority. I pay close attention to my feelings about my boss, my minister or any professional. If someone abuses power I can protect myself. If I become unreasonably defiant I will gently and firmly reassure my inner child.

Today I will respond rationally to authority and I will assert my own authority responsibly.

I am connected to the earth and the sky.

My inner child is connected to both the earth and the sky. I close my eyes and see my inner child and myself walking slowly, peacefully through a forest. The sun's rays pour through the branches, dappling the ground with pools of light. We breathe deeply, enjoying the smell of trees and leaves, the soil under our feet. We walk until we see a tree we both like. We put our arms around it in a wide embrace, feeling the tree's calm strength penetrate deeply into our bodies. This tree takes its time with life, it's not going anywhere. It's content to grow, nourished by the earth and the sun.

We close our eyes and pretend we are trees. We feel our feet grow roots that sink deep into the earth, tapping natural fresh water springs. We absorb the water into our bodies, feel it flowing up, as our hands and arms become branches, reaching for the sun. We breathe in and out, secure between the earth and the sky.

Today I will strengthen my spiritual powers with the courage of my adolescence.

Maya Angelou writes about adolescents, "Few, if any, survive their teens. Most surrender to the vague but murderous pressure of adult conformity."

There is something very valiant in teenagers' struggles to grow up in our culture. They must fight for their spiritual life and they find an inner courage that, in their adult life, may astonish them. They confront old labels and limits within the family and society and they dare to be different.

In a certain way, teenagers create role models for their future adult selves. In my family of origin, my conflicts were unacknowledged or discounted as "mere rebellion." As an adult child, I forgot the image of my teenaged spiritual warrior.

Today I will dare to be different. I will strengthen my spiritual powers with the courage of my adolescence.

I have all the time I need.

Sometimes I feel as though I'll never have enough time to do all the things I need to do.

Today I will live in "child time," when school threatened to drag on forever and summer promised to never end. In this time of long, full, wonderful days, I can begin to slow down and look closely at everything. I can lie in the grass and watch as a whole world opens to me. From this perspective, I see ants marching home carrying grains of soil that seem the size of boulders, weeds that look like redwood trees, and spider webs that resemble fishing nets. When I tire of this view, I can roll over and look up in the sky, watching the clouds slowly pass, changing shape from ship to castle to wisp.

Today, in child time, I will see things I have never noticed, even though they have always been there. I *do* have the time.

I am healing the shame of my inner child.

Today I will seek to love the little one within. I want to help heal him of the shame he carries. I will describe all the special qualities I see in him — his intelligence, sense of humor, curiosity and kindheartedness.

The messages I received growing up in my dysfunctional family left me feeling shameful about my identity. I never received the unconditional love that would have reassured me that I was an acceptable person. Consequently, I have spent my whole life trying to hide my shame, behind a facade. I submerged myself in my work or in a relationship or in the role of parent. I threw myself into the pursuit of perfection, seeking to bury my inner shame beneath a flurry of activity.

Yet as I have grown to love and respect myself more, I clearly see how destructive it is to avoid my shame by running from it. Today I will remove the facade and speak to my inner child. "You are a beloved child of God. You don't have to hide from anyone any more."

**Today I will trust my Higher Power
to guide me.**

Winnie the Pooh, on a blustery day, found himself pinned beneath some furniture when the world seemed to turn upside down. While waiting for the storm to stop, he wrote a little song to help pass the time in a pleasant fashion.

Storms of rage and self-hatred blow into my life, turning everything I've worked for upside down. My thoughts and emotions battle for control, leaving me feeling quite hopeless. The harder I try, the stronger the storms grow.

Perhaps I cannot always dispel the storms. Some storms must be lived through. So today I will choose to write my own song of sorts. I may take a walk in the park. I may vent my feelings to a trusted friend. I may run, swim or ride a bike. Through it all, I will trust my Higher Power to hold me up and keep me from drowning. In the end, the storm will be a blessing, for I will learn something of lasting value.

I am the source of validation
for my inner child.

Today I will celebrate my recovery by eliminating the need to take hostages in relationships.

Fear prompts me to control and cling to those closest to me. This fear emanates from the desperate child within me who is afraid of being hurt. Yet controlling and clinging only drive away our loved ones and make our worst fears come true. Now I know that when I feel tempted to lose myself in a relationship, my inner child is yearning for the parental approval she never received. I am her source of validation, not anyone else.

When I give my inner child the love and nurturing she craves and deserves, her death grip on other people loosens. Today I will stop controlling and allow my loved ones to be themselves.

I can confront what frightens me.

For too long now I have behaved like a fearful child hiding behind his mother's skirts. I have let my fears rule my life, preventing me from doing what my heart tells me to do. I use my fear as a way to protect myself from things I do not want to face.

Today I will no longer close my eyes to things I do not want to see. I am ready to open my eyes and, with a calm steady gaze, confront the heart of the beast. I am surprised by what I see. It is not the horrible monster I was expecting. Instead I see a lost, lonely, frightened child, a part of myself left out in the cold for too long. I ask him what he wants from me and he replies, "I only want to be let in, clothed, fed and kept warm."

I take him in my arms and say, "Don't be afraid. You're with me now." I feel my fear crumble between my fingers like dry paper and blow away.

**I have my own unique gifts to
give to the world.**

I want to be a fiction writer and to sing on stage. I want to be an actress and to be known as a wise old sage. I want to make people laugh, to travel far and near. I want to be so many things but now it's very clear. I will never be Dickens or Caruso, Bernhardt or King Solomon. There is only one Chevy Chase and, thankfully, only one me.

I can bless the world with my gifts and talents whatever they may be. The child within has many gifts to offer. I may have the gift of friendship, listening or hospitality. I may gift my employer with my unfailing ability. Or I may convince some friends to do volunteer work, using my gift of gab.

Perhaps it is my smile that boosts another's self-esteem or my hug that holds another's loneliness at bay. I'm very much . . . a gifted, talented, special person.

**I am a loving and responsive parent
to my inner child.**

We learn to treat ourselves the way we were
treated. Because I grew up with constant nega-
tion, I learned to treat myself abusively. There
was no room for error in my home. Now in my
internal home I use shaming self-talk that mu-
tilates the spirit of my inner child. No wonder
my inner child is hesitant to show herself. In
order to heal my wounded spirit, I must make
some different choices.

So today I choose to be a loving and responsive
parent to my inner child. I understand and
accept that I can't always be perfect or do the
"right" thing. I know that growing up is difficult
and I guide my inner child as best I can. I do
not need to scold or abuse her. I am aware that
she is young and vulnerable and I give her my
unconditional and everflowing love.

Today I envision a life of happiness.

Today I will use my imagination to visualize blessings in my life instead of catastrophe. When my inner child reacts in fear, I will gently reassure her by deliberately fixing my imagination on scenes of goodness and hope.

Throughout the chaotic years in my dysfunctional home, I became quite skilled at visualizing imaginary scenes in my mind. Unfortunately, the scenes I imagined usually reflected the atmosphere of fear in my home. The fears of my inner child are still with me. They provide the dark materials for my imagination to dwell upon. Often I become obsessed with thoughts of disaster.

Today I will consciously focus on thoughts of blessings and future health. I will envision a life of happiness for myself in every aspect.

**Today I look forward to a rich and
rewarding old age.**

Today I will look forward to growing older. Just
as I value the richness of my inner child's
growth, so, too, do I value the promise of the
growth to come in old age.

While growing up, I absorbed the negative
messages about aging fed to me by my culture
and my family. I equated strength and self-
worth with youthful vigor and attractiveness.
My attempts to look younger than my years
served only to accentuate my fear.

Now I can look all around me and find role
models in seniors who join the Peace Corps,
write novels or run a marathon. Today I will
envision myself in vigorous old age, serving as
a role model for all my juniors. I know that I
will never stop growing.

> **I play many roles and my
> identity is congruent.**

As a child I didn't like pretending to be someone else, nor did I want my friends to be anything other than who they were. I was scared by all the masks. Would I know my friends behind their masks? Would they know me?

As an adult, I now understand that we all wear masks sometimes. We have a social mask, a work mask, a school mask, a child mask, a parent mask. Yet underneath these masks is our real face, the face that never changes. When I observe myself taking off one mask and putting on another, it reminds me of the way I change clothes for different occasions. I wear my masks comfortably, knowing it is me who speaks through them. Always mindful of the real person underneath my mask, I am not frightened of the social mask of others.

I can create a satisfying social life.

I will celebrate my attractiveness as a person by creating a satisfying social life for myself. Outings, parties and entertainment in the company of others can enrich my life.

Social life was virtually nonexistent when I was a child. Inwardly consumed by their own pain and shame, my addicted parents isolated themselves from the rest of the world. Because life at home was too unpredictable, I rarely risked inviting any of my friends to visit me. As a result, I grew to adulthood without any real experience of a normal, satisfying social life. I often spent my leisure time alone because social events were simply too uncomfortable for me.

As I grow toward wholeness, I feel the desire to be with others. I find that enjoying the company of friends fills deep needs in my soul. Today I will go about the business of creating a satisfying social life.

I can ask for help to parent my inner child.

Sometimes the task of nurturing my inner child makes me feel like a single parent, overwhelmed by the enormity of it all. My inner child needs so much love, so much help, so much encouragement. I wonder if I'm really equipped to give him all he deserves. Sometimes I feel like giving up. I want to throw up my hands and cry, "I just can't do it." I want to scream and rage at him to leave me alone. I need help.

In recovery, I am learning to ask for help with parenting my inner child. I can ask for support from friends, from counselors, from my wise inner self. I am not alone. Others have gone through this before me and others are in the midst of it now. I do not have to berate myself for feeling tired — this is hard work.

Today I will ask for help and accept it with gratitude.

I will be fully present today.

As a child growing up in a chaotic family, I learned to go numb when bad things happened. I escaped into a fantasy world where I could have control and not be afraid. This survival mechanism served me well as a child but chokes my spirit as an adult.

I realize that I need to be fully present to experience life. Instead of viewing life from a distance, I need to take risks, cultivate eccentricity and open myself to my feelings. As I get closer to finding my true essence, my life becomes worth living and I can be proud of it.

Whatever I do today is important because I am exchanging a day of my life for it. Today I will coax myself into action. I will express my talents and capabilities as I allow myself to experience life.

**I release my inner child from the task
of knowing everything.**

My inner child is an investigator. Asking questions is a major part of growing-up. What, who, when, why, how, how long? Each question is valid. Answers may not always be available, but questions are the beginning of knowledge and wisdom.

Growing up in my dysfunctional family, I had to guess a lot of the time. Questions were dangerous so I learned to ask as few as possible. There still exists an inner child who is afraid to ask questions. In a group of people, I still become shameful when I don't understand what is being discussed. I still experience the fear of being exposed as stupid or inadequate.

Today I will release myself from the impossible task of knowing everything. I will ask questions at work and at home, gathering information instead of making assumptions.

Today I will make up my own mind.

Today I will affirm that I am capable of making up my own mind. I know what I want to do and I can act on it. I can look at a situation calmly, consider the alternatives and choose the correct course. My judgment is sound.

I will no longer worry about whether or not I am doing the right thing or about what others will say or think of me. I do not have to become obsessed with the dilemma of making a decision, wondering which is the perfect choice. I will not ruminate over whether I have picked the wrong one and if disaster is to follow. Today I will simply choose, knowing I have carefully thought my decision through.

I rejoice in my ability to make a conscious decision. I feel clear, competent and strong. With each decision I make, I grow in confidence that the next will be easier.

My inner child heals through grieving.

Today I will accept my inner child's sadness. Occasional bouts of melancholy are my inner child's way of healing through grieving. I will not fear this feeling when it comes; I may cry, for tears often cleanse the soul of its residue of sadness.

As an adult child, I may always feel a lingering depression. There may always be a "hole" inside me that nothing can quite fill. Maturity means coming to accept life on its own terms — even if that entails learning to live with a sense of loss — without concluding that there's something "wrong" with me.

The child within me was told that sadness was unacceptable. Today I will allow him the freedom to feel sad. As he grieves, I will love and comfort him. Despite the losses of yesterday, this day glistens before me with all the rich hues of hope and promise.

I acknowledge my dark past and create a bright future.

An unseen hand draws a black curtain across the summer sky, slowly, as if hating to see the day come to an end. Pinholes alter the blackness with tiny spots of sparkling lights. I lean back to marvel at the pinholes in the black curtain. Each time I look, I see something different. Feelings sweep over me. Sometimes tears even trickle down my face at the beauty of the simplicity.

Just like the night sky, my childhood is cloaked with a black curtain. Now pinholes of light create beauty out of ugliness. Past hurts can now be used for something positive. I can reach out to comfort others who have the same hurts because I know how it feels. I can make changes within myself that will, in turn, alter the dynamics in my new world of relationships.

The curtain does not always have to be dark. Today I can, and I will, create beautiful patterns of light for others to see and appreciate.

I will open my senses today.

Today is a day to revel in my sensual being. I participate in life today with my senses open, alert and receptive.

So often as I was growing up in my alcoholic family, I found my vision clouded, my hearing stunned and my sense of touch turned numb.

Today I will take special care to open my eyes to the beauty of nature, to the nebulous, free-form artistry of clouds, to the wizardry of trees and leaves. I see colors, shapes and shades.

I listen to sounds, to the murmur of voices, the mood of music, and the hushed flow of air. I taste flavors and I savor my food, my sustenance. I touch those near to me with love and gentleness and am touched in turn. I cherish the texture of touch, the texture of life.

I can say no.

When I was a child, I was afraid to say no. I saw my parents withdraw their love and attention when I was not compliant. I truly believed kids who said, "If you don't do such and such, I won't be your friend anymore." As I grew up, I harbored more and more resentment and continued to let others determine my limits. I have spent far too much of my life agreeing to do unpleasant things just because I was afraid of not being loved.

In my recovery, I no longer am paralyzed with fear. I *can* say no. I believe in my own wisdom, my own rights, my own ability to make decisions that are right for me. I know that a friend who threatens to leave me if I disagree, was never my friend at all. My real friends support my right to make decisions in my own best interest.

I am finding my own integrity.

The child within asks, "Who am I really?"

In my family of origin, I played the inappropriate role of caretaker. As a child, I could not refuse this role but inside I felt hollow and dishonest. I also observed my parents denying their alcoholism and disguising their reality in public. Their behavior at home was often violent and bizarre and I felt confused and angry.

Today I am finding my own integrity. At work, at home, with friends in the community, I am authentic and congruent. Through my recovery, I can distinguish between appropriate roles and dishonest behavior.

I am gradually replacing my cynicism with trust in my genuine self.

I patiently await the fruits of my self-love.

When I was five years old, I planted my first garden. I planted the seeds, covered them with soil, watered them every day and waited for them to grow. I became so impatient for them to sprout that I dug them up to see what was happening. There, on each little seed, I saw the beginnings of green.

I learned that each seed knew exactly how much time it needed to take root in the soil. Hidden underground each was growing, becoming what it was meant to be.

Today I allow my own seeds of change to grow silently and invisibly. I water them well and give them all the nourishment they need. I am patient in the knowledge that, with my care, they will take root. I allow them to germinate in peace, without disturbance, until I see the first green shoot pushing triumphantly into the light. With every first bloom, I will reap the fruits of my self-love.

I weave the pattern of my life.

I weave the pattern of my life. I hold the threads, I choose the colors, I put them on the loom in the pattern of my choosing.

When I make a mistake, I do not scold myself for being a bad weaver. Nor do I rip out my work in anger and frustration. I rejoice, because each mistake gives me the opportunity to create a pattern that is uniquely mine, rich with the turnings and twistings of my life.

My work will never be finished but will grow ever richer and more beautiful.

I am content to grow at my own pace.

Some babies crawl when they are five months old. Some do not crawl until much later. Some babies are petite, some are husky. Some are placid, content to gurgle and coo. Others are active, forever reaching for this toy or that. If allowed to be themselves, babies will grow at their own pace. Comparisons are needless, for when they become adults no one will know whether they crawled early or late, were petite or husky, were placid or active.

I, too, can grow at my own pace, without comparing myself with others. I accept that there will always be those who grow faster and those who grow slower than I. Who I am and what I am are no longer conditional on my rate of growth. Today I will continue to take one step at a time, enjoying the pace set by my inner child.

My inner child has the run of the house.

In my childhood home, the living room rug was white and the furniture was covered with plastic, which was removed only for company, adult company. My rigid, perfectionistic parents made it clear that I was supposed to stay out of the living room, no matter what. They demanded that I keep my room as neat as a pin. My parents' house was for adults only. There was no place for me.

Today my inner child has the run of the house. He is free to enjoy every room. He has his own space where he can do whatever he likes. He also helps keep the rest of the house in order because he enjoys the peacefulness that order brings. We have comfortable furniture that forgives the mistakes of young and old alike. We live together in comfort and harmony. We both belong here.

I am empowered to heal the painful parts of my life.

My life as a child was very painful. To survive, I constructed a reality for myself built on wishes. After a while I began to live as if my fantasy were real. Living in a fantasy allowed me to deny some truths about my life.

It's time now to stop pretending. I know that if I continue to pretend things are better or different than they really are, I will never resolve my hurt. By living in fantasy, I only put off my grieving. I will continue to experience pain as long as I live in my expectations instead of my reality.

I am strong enough now to accept the difference between fantasy and reality. I can acknowledge and confront my pain, past and present. My acceptance of my reality empowers me to heal the painful parts of my life.

I will take the pressure off myself.

"Do more!" "Accomplish more!" These messages from my childhood have driven me all my life. As a child, I could never do enough to please my parents. The standards they set were always higher than those I had already achieved. The core of these messages was that I wasn't good enough as I was. I had to do more and be more to be acceptable. Yet no one is standing over me demanding that I do more. Now the pressure that I'm under is pressure that I am putting on myself.

Today I will break this vicious cycle before I blow like the engine of a race car pushed far beyond its limits. I will reassure my inner child that she is wonderful just the way she is; she has nothing to prove to anyone any longer. Today I will take the pressure off myself and experience the wonderful freedom of being human, not a machine.

Today I will allow myself the freedom to be.

Consider the wildflowers. They do not work hard to be beautiful. They do not strive for a place in the meadow or on the hill. They simply are. My inner child needs to be appreciated for being, not just for doing.

I have spent much of my life in busy preparation. All the commotion is designed to keep me moving, to keep me from failing, maybe even to keep me from remembering or feeling. For at least one hour today I will consider the wildflowers. Perhaps I will lie in a meadow or on a hill or in my own backyard with a book. Then I will allow myself to be like the wildflowers. Not striving or frantic, just being. If being brings memories of painful feelings, they can come to visit but I will not allow them to stay and destroy the flowers.

Today I will allow myself the freedom to be the best of my God-given gifts, *me*.

I allow my trust to grow gradually.

As a child, my parents fought day after day. I heard their screams and insults, intercepted their dirty looks and witnessed their marriage come to an end.

The marriage between my distrusting parents is the one and only relationship that I have taken to heart. Now, as an adult, I have no trust in any kind of loving relationship.

Today I will start fresh with a frame of mind that will grow broader and broader each day. I will not jump aimlessly into any relationship, at any cost. Instead I will concentrate on gradually getting to know a new special friend, not trusting wholly but letting my trust and the trust between us grow along with our relationship. In this way I may not fall in love but grow into love.

I can choose rules that enhance my life.

As a child, others made rules for me. My teachers told me when to stand up, when to sit down, when to do my school work. My parents told me when to sleep, what to eat, when to play.

Today I will carefully assess the rules that govern my life. If they fit, I can choose to keep them. If they do not, I can discard or modify them. I no longer have to obey my parents.

I will create my own set of rules using this criterion: Does this rule or guideline enhance my life and enable me to be a more creative and fulfilled person? Or does it constrict my life and keep me bound to my past?

Today I will discard rules from my past and choose guidelines with which I can feel comfortable.

I acknowledge my gifts.

The child within me is gifted and creative. I accept my talents as gifts from my Higher Power and claim creativity as my birthright.

In my dysfunctional family, my gifts were unacknowledged or hidden as shameful secrets. My creative energy was harnessed only to serve the needs of my parents.

Today I will claim my creativity, knowing that my gifts belong to me. These gifts were given to me so I could fulfill my desires and my purpose in this world. It is through my creativity that I express my God-self.

As I share my creativity with the world, I am energized. I delight in the spark of creativity within that is ignited by the spirit of my inner child.

I respect the wisdom of my child spirit.

My child spirit is flying a kite. A kite depends on the wind for lift. I can run and run and run and never get it up in the air. Yet with just a breath of wind, whoosh and up it goes.

An experienced kite-flier now, I never waste my time running in circles on still days. I sit quietly, enjoying the stillness. When I feel the air start to move, I'm ready. I let out some string and my kite climbs higher and higher, until it's almost out of sight. I play with the balance: If I let the string go slack, the kite will fly away forever. If I pull too hard, it will tumble down to the ground. If I keep some tension on the string, the kite soars and glides and loops until I bring it down.

My inner child inherently knows the balance between holding on and letting go. I know I need to learn both to have healthy intimate relationships. Today I will remember the feeling of flying a kite. I will respect the wisdom of my inner child.

Today I will follow the rules of natural order.

The world is an orderly place. Day follows night, season follows season. Every living thing exists within the rules of a natural order.

Nature provides signals that help all living things follow the rules of survival. In spring, leaves "read" a light signal that tells the plant to flower. Sometimes nature gives more than one signal so that a plant does not sprout on a warm autumn day before the winter frost.

As a child, I did not learn to read the signals of my physical needs. I learned not to feel hunger or tiredness, so I did not eat or rest at the proper times.

In recovery, I am learning to read the signals of my body. Now I respond early rather than waiting for a growling stomach or extreme fatigue. Today I will structure my day around the needs of my body. I will follow the rules of natural order.

I can be who I am without shame.

I feel the exhilarating freedom today of letting my inner self be reflected in my outer self. I can be myself around others without the slightest shame, for I am a wonderful person.

The wounded child within me is deathly afraid to reveal who he really is. The shaming messages of childhood still terrorize him: "You're worthless! You're no good!" He is convinced that if anyone discovered who he really is, he would be rejected.

As an adult in recovery, I now realize that my fears are not based on reality. I have selected friends who know the real me and I am still loved and accepted.

Today I will give up the time-consuming addiction of creating a false image. I love who I am and will live as I am today without shame.

Today I choose to laugh!

Too often I take life too seriously. There wasn't much laughter in my childhood. Misery is so comfortable that I sometimes create a crisis where there is none.

Today I will focus on laughter. Perhaps I'll rent a funny movie and invite a lighthearted friend over to watch it with me.

Laughter does not mean I am denying my painful past. Laughter means I see the future from a new perspective, understanding it is my choice to be happy or unhappy. I will let my happy child within emerge today to rekindle my playful spirit. My past may affect my future but it does not govern it.

The choices I make today will determine my future. And today I choose to laugh.

I pay attention to my feelings.

I need to pay attention to my feelings instead of cutting them off. It's important for me to take my feelings seriously. Am I sad? Happy? Yearning? Angry?

As a child, I was taught to deny my feelings. My anger was bad, it might hurt someone. I shouldn't be too happy, I might be disappointed. Don't be sad, think of something nice. Constantly bombarded by messages to deny, I found it easier and safer to shut off my feelings than to explore them.

Now there is a big part of me that I don't know or understand. Paying attention to my feelings can help me open that door.

My emotions are fluid and they lead me inward to the source of my wisdom and power.

I am discovering my passion for learning.

As a child, the month of September meant the beginning of school. I was always excited to see all my friends but dreaded the confining walls that kept me imprisoned nine months a year. I listened to teachers lecture hour after hour. I longed to get out and explore my world — to see, touch, smell and experiment with my environment. My love of learning was diminished and I began to associate learning with boredom.

Now as an adult, it's time to change my beliefs. I understand that painful school experiences can cause feelings of low self-esteem that last a lifetime. Just because my method of learning was different from others does not mean I am stupid. Today I will learn one new thing about the world — and I will learn it my way. I will visit a museum, read a book, listen to a tape or talk to friends. My inner child is alive with curiosity as I discover my passion for learning.

I ask for help when I need it.

When I was about five years old, I decided that asking for help was a babyish thing to do, a sign of weakness. I thought I had to figure everything out for myself. I didn't want anyone to think I wasn't smart or resourceful. As a consequence, there are a lot of things I never learned or half-learned or learned wrong.

Now I know that my inner child doesn't have all the answers and neither do I. Today I will retrace my steps and find out what I need to know. Then I will seek out the people who can help me. Working together, we will arrive at the answer much more quickly and surely than I ever could alone.

I accept my authority and the authority of others.

As an adult child, I tend to feel uncomfortable about my authority or react negatively to the legitimate authority of others. In a dysfunctional family, authority is not based on rational grounds or reasonable actions. My parents confused power with control and their self-respect was based on my obedience or approval.

In recovery, I acknowledge my right to exercise authority over my thoughts and actions. I responsibly perform the roles of parent and worker, and I practice detachment in separating my responsibility from the responsibility of others. Today I will accept my authority and the legitimate authority of others.

I am strong inside.

When I was very small, life was a frightening place. The only way I could protect myself was to build walls around me — from the anger of parents, from the taunts of friends, from the unknown terrors the world holds for a small child. Inside those walls I was safe. So I learned to live inside that tiny, airless, constricted space.

I lived within my walls for so long that I forgot the reason for their existence, and even that it was I who had erected them.

Now I know that I don't need that artificial shell because I am strong *inside*. I no longer see the tiny child who was cowering in fear. I see that child bursting free, radiating strength from inside out. Utilizing my courage and my strength, I see my walls fall one by one.

I can break my habit of lying.

Today I will leave behind the web of unnecessary lies that has woven itself into the fabric of my life.

Lying was an integral part of my life as a child. I lied to my friends to hide my shame about my dysfunctional family. I lied to my parents to protect myself from their anger and disapproval. Worse, I learned to lie to myself about my childhood and my family.

Lying became a habit. Some lies were destructive to me as, one by one, I used them to build a fortress of denial. Some were simply unnecessary lies, born of habit.

Now I must break this habit, for it hinders my recovery. By accepting and telling the truth, I can free my inner child from the shame she feels for having been forced to lie to survive.

Today I will set myself free by being honest with others — and with myself.

Today I will exercise as an act of self-love.

Today I will give my body the exercise it needs to be strong, flexible and healthy.

In my dysfunctional home, no one taught me to value my body. It was either a source of shame to be ignored or merely a prop to be used for seduction, manipulation or achievement. The idea of taking care of my body was totally foreign to me. In fact, I had to ignore most of the cues my body gave me in order to survive in my home. As an adult, I still escape my body by not taking care of it: layering it with fat or starving it into oblivion. One way to feel my physical essence again is to exercise.

I will exercise today as an act of self-love. Because I have grown to value my body, I will not be compulsive in my exercise or drive my body beyond its limits. Instead, I will begin with a mild workout that leaves me deeply relaxed and glowing with vitality.

I can ask for affection without being sexually provocative.

I can ask for affection without being sexually provocative. My need for love and warmth is not tied to my sexual desires. I do not have to sleep with people in order for them to be my friends. I have a right to be held and nurtured without "paying" for it by making love.

In the past, I could never seem to get close to someone without being sexual. Hugs and kisses automatically meant sex and I went along with it, not knowing any other way to get what I needed. The emptiness I felt would temporarily be soothed by sexual encounters. But I wound up feeling shameful and unsatisfied.

Now I can drop the lure of sex and ask for what I really need: love, affection, warmth, closeness. I deserve to be loved unconditionally.

I allow myself to be healed.

When I am hurt and in pain, I allow myself to be healed. I no longer have to suffer. Suffering is *not* good for the soul. I do not have to show my scars to all, demanding sympathy and offering them up as excuses for my behavior.

I open myself to the idea of healing, and its power is with me everywhere. As I drink a glass of water, I say, "Let the healing spirit of this water cleanse my body of impurity." As I take my first breath of air in the morning, I say, "I inhale all the healing energy of the morning and exhale yesterday's negativity." As I take a bath, I immerse myself in the healing energy of the water, allowing it to wash away all impurities of body, mind and soul.

Today I will give myself an opportunity to be healed.

Today I will be the leader in my own life.

Today I will allow myself to know what makes me happy.

In school I was always the follower, never the leader. I felt safe doing what everyone else wanted to do. I never asked myself what *I* wanted to do. Letting others make my decisions for me was a relief. I thought I would make them happy if I agreed with their plans.

I grew up to be an adult who lived the lives of others. Because I never asked myself what my needs were, I denied that I had any needs at all.

Today I will let my inner child be the leader, knowing I have the answers to my questions: "What do I want to do today?" "What do I need for myself?" "What do I need from my family and friends?" Today I will lead my own life.

**I can shrink the bullies in my life
down to size.**

Today I will refuse to feel small and powerless when confronted by bullies who would
abuse me.

I learned to feel powerless growing up in my
dysfunctional family. My parents' needs came
first, mine last. I felt controlled, either by their
threats or by their manipulative conditional
love. Gradually, I came to believe that I had no
personal power.

Now I know that although the child within me
has remained small, I have grown up. I have
learned through the give-and-take of adult life
that I am powerful, and that my needs are
important.

When confronted with controlling or abusive
behavior, I will summon my power and my
courage. Today I will not be intimidated by
controlling or abusive behavior.

Today I will set the course of my life.

Today I will determine my own course in life. I'll get a good map and a compass to show me the right direction and seek out good companions on my way. I may look at the map of life and decide where I want to go or simply explore all the avenues that are open to me.

I am no longer lost in a dark fairy-tale forest filled with wolves and witches waiting to get me. Like the proverbial youngest son, I am ready for the journey: I have my cake for sustenance, and I can find others to share it with me. I have my wits about me and the courage to persevere. I am not sure where I'll end up, but I know that my journey will be a wonderful adventure.

Today I will rejoice in my own giftedness.

Some people are more gifted than others. Too often I look to those more richly gifted than I and place them on a higher plane of worthiness. Instead of seeing myself as gifted, I often see myself as being limited. In my family I was often unfavorably compared with others. As a child, I strived hard, working endlessly to be what I was not.

Today I look to the musicians in a symphony orchestra. There are many cellists, many flutists, many violinists. Some play their instruments with more grace and precision than others do. Yet all are needed.

Today I will rejoice in my own giftedness. I will appreciate others and their gifts without devaluing myself and my own gifts.

I express my emotions freely.

Sometimes my inner child is a whining kid. It drives me crazy to listen to that seemingly endless whine. It reminds me of the screechy sound air makes when it is slowly, slowly released from a balloon. I think whining is the sound that anger makes when it's not allowed to speak freely. Even though the whining eventually ceases a little, anger remains to fuel the next whine.

Today I will remind my inner child of the balloon. "Watch this," I say, as I blow a balloon up as big as it can get and let it go. The balloon flies wildly around the room for an instant and then drops to the floor, its energy spent.

I tell my inner child, "Try to be like that balloon. Don't be afraid to let your anger out freely. You may fly around the room for a moment but soon your anger will subside and you can rest."

**Today I will applaud the genius
of my inner child.**

My intelligence shines brightly within me and
sheds light on the world about me.

As a child from a dysfunctional family, I did not
have the energy to think clearly or to pursue
my interests. I applied my intelligence to finding survival strategies, and I developed my
reason in an attempt to adapt to the irrational
behaviors of my family.

As part of my recovery, I choose to uncover
new interests and release my energy to pursue
these interests. I may spend a whole day in a
library and check out stacks of books on leaves,
fashions, astrophysics, pop songs, auto repair. I
may sign up for a class or volunteer for a neigh-
borhood project.

Today I will apply my reasoning power to my
recovery. I will applaud the curiosity and genius
of my inner child.

I am open to the beauty that surrounds me.

Let gentleness govern my life today. Casting aside my protective shell, my muscles loosen and I become less rigid, less brittle.

It's easier to smile as I move in harmony with nature. My spirit flows from moment to moment. When I am tender and gentle to myself, I become aware of the gentleness in others.

Like a toddler exploring the world for the first time, I delight in all that is around me. All things become new. I reach out to touch the bark of a tree, the fur of the neighbor's cat, the face of a friend. I am touched by soft currents of air. I listen for faint sounds and take delight in subtle tastes and smells.

The here and now is my present. Past pain and fear are put aside. I eagerly open my arms to the beauty that surrounds me from moment to moment.

I allow my inner child to be himself.

When I was a child, I tried to please others, to anticipate their needs, to be all that I thought they wanted me to be. Like a chameleon, I could change at will, depending on whom I was with and what I assumed that person would like best. I was proud of this ability but it also terrified me. I didn't know who I really was, or if there was anyone inside me at all.

Today I allow my inner child to be himself. I respect his individuality, his wants and needs, his talents and his limitations. I hold his thoughts, ideas, goals and discoveries in high regard. I will allow and encourage him to look within to find and respect his uniqueness. He is no longer invisible to others. He is a real person in his own right. I delight in making his acquaintance and I trust that others will like and respect him as I do.

I will make the most of each opportunity.

A new door unexpectedly opens in my life. It leads to choices and possibilities I never before considered. Even though it is open, I hesitate. Going through the door might mean a whole change of life. It might mean disaster. It might even mean adventure.

The unpredictability of my childhood made me fear change. It left me with a need for everything always to be the same. It made me want to close my eyes and run past open doors of opportunity.

Today I will no longer let the dysfunction of my childhood keep me blind to the possibilities of life. I will let my toddler within explore what lies beyond the door. I will make the most of every opportunity put in my path. I may find the door leads exactly where I intended to go.

I am creating my own rules.

My values create the foundation for healthy choices. I am learning the difference between adapting to another's expectations to feel accepted and experimenting with different rules to find out what fits for me.

There are many times in my adulthood when I feel like I never left adolescence. When I encounter different social or professional situations, I become awkward and uncertain. I sometimes feel shameful — thinking that everyone else must know the rules — except me.

In my recovery, I am establishing my own values. I have a right to choose work and relationships that complement my values. If I am unsure about the rules in any situation, I can ask questions or form my own.

Today I will I create rules that work for me.

Today I will comfort my inner child.

As a child, thunderstorms or howling snow-storms scared me. Often there was no one to comfort me. I was either shamed for being afraid or bribed with food to be quiet. There still exists within me a scared little child who panics during storms, a child who needs com-forting and reassurance.

Today I will remind my child that changes in the weather are only God appearing to me in different forms. I will hold my child gently in my thoughts and remind her that lightning will not strike her dead, that she is not going to be punished for being a bad girl.

I am learning to be a nurturing parent to my inner child.

I will speak up for my rights.

I do not need to feel trapped — in relationships, in my career, or in any other life circumstance. I have been given all the abilities I need to create an enjoyable life for myself.

My needs didn't count when I was a child. I stuffed my feelings and my needs and didn't talk about them. I was trapped in a destructive situation as a child and I still feel trapped as an adult. Yet I have come to see that the reason I feel trapped is my desire to avoid confrontation. My inner child is afraid that if she expresses her needs directly, she will be abandoned. As a result, I have remained in self-destructive situations.

Today I will break this cycle. I do not have to accept less than the best for myself. I deserve to be treated with respect. A surge of relief sweeps through me as I begin to take control of my own destiny.

I am a sexual being.

I am a sexual being. I have the right to express and explore my sexuality. I feel the fiery sexual energy warming and empowering me. I no longer have to hide my body's sexuality in loose clothes or flaunt it in too-tight clothes or be ashamed of its very existence.

I radiate sexuality. I am aware of its power and I use power lovingly and respectfully.

My sexuality connects me with the essence of all life: the generative power of the earth itself.

I am overcoming my praise deficit.

Just as a marathon runner experiences an oxygen deficit after miles of exertion so, too, did I develop a praise deficit while growing up. I yearned to be appreciated. Yet because I received so little recognition from my parents, I began to question whether I was a good person worthy of praise.

In my adult life, I have sought to fill my praise deficit by fishing for compliments. At times, I have manipulated others into praising me by expressing false humility.

Today I will give up these false ways of filling my praise deficit. I will fill my mind with positive self-talk. I will start keeping a journal in which I can jot down a list of my daily triumphs, great and small.

Today I will meet my needs for praise without resorting to manipulation.

Today I will start to dream again.

An eight-year-old sits in school staring out of the window. Once again he's daydreaming. Maybe tonight Dad will come home happy and we'll have fun like we used to. Time after time he is disappointed.

Dreams often die young in families who hide alcoholism. I stopped dreaming many years ago, for my dreams never came true. Usually the very opposite happened. I was ridiculed for having dreams. Soon I learned that dreams are ridiculous. They involve a positive outlook and unfathomable possibilities. I had no time for such foolishness.

Today I will start to dream again. I will dare to think the impossible. I will allow myself to laugh about it, get excited about it and fantasize about all the things it could entail.

I affirm myself with words of respect.

My past can be a lethal poison. A healing antidote is affirmation. I could wait until others provide the affirmations I need. Better yet, I could take responsibility for my own healing.

From this day forward, I will affirm myself with words of respect. My words will be based not on what I do but on who I am. As I reflect on the God-given qualities that are unique to me, I will speak them aloud to myself.

"I appreciate my kindness." "My gentleness is calming to others." "Sometimes it is hard to be honest but my integrity is honorable."

I will continuously replace the words of rejection from my past with words of affirmation beginning today.

I allow people to be who they are.

Today I will revel in the freedom of letting others do what they want and be who they are. I no longer need to insist that everyone do things my way.

The angry frightened 10-year-old within me never learned to negotiate from a position of power. She always felt powerless and fighting back by demanding her own way was her survival technique. This defensive stance has outlived its usefulness in my adult life. I am far enough along on my path toward recovery to know that I have power over my destiny. I can create solutions to meet my needs without violating anyone else's boundaries. I no longer need to manipulate others. Today I will pursue my happiness instead of insisting that others do things my way.

I enjoy being silly.

I grew up with the idea that life is serious business. My parents were quick to point out, "If you're going to get somewhere, stick to the straight and narrow and don't take time out for any silliness." I learned to face life with grim forebearance, to be prepared for the hardships that were sure to come my way. My perception of life has turned out to be a self-fulfilling prophecy: The grimmer I think life will be, the grimmer it gets.

Today I will allow my inner child to be silly. I feel lighter with the realization that I can have fun today. I will take some time off today to run on the beach, jump in puddles or play in the park. I may tell silly jokes or make funny faces at myself in the mirror. I will enjoy the shock on people's faces that know me as sullen and predictable.

My world looks brighter as I experiment with being outrageous.

I am developing my personal philosophy.

I will take another step toward self-respect and self-affirmation today by developing my personal philosophy of life. As a child, I was never encouraged to think independently. Even as an adult, I allowed my partner and others to dictate their philosophy to me. Beneath my passive acceptance of others' views was my secret conviction that I was incapable of developing a valid philosophy of my own.

In recovery, I have come to appreciate the good mind I have been given. I have excellent insights and a perspective on life worthy of respect. Most of all, I possess life experiences. Some were successes, some were failures. All were valuable lessons.

Today I will honor my intelligence and my life experiences by formulating my own philosophy of life.

I can set my own limits.

Today I will trust myself to set my own limits. I will climb as high as I can safely climb. I will walk as far as it is safe to go. I will find the edge and stop there. I will take only as many steps as I can manage.

Within these bounds, I am free to run, jump and spin. I shout for joy at my accomplishment and so does my inner child.

I know exactly how far I can go today. Tomorrow I can go a little further.

I can change the way I view my past.

Today I will reach down into the dark depths of my soul and bring the most painful scenes out into the light where I can view them through adult eyes. I see desperately miserable parents lashing out at their innocent child. I see school children mocking cruelly, their name-calling creating wounds that weren't deserved.

As I see these hurts through new eyes, the labels of shame I had allowed to be attached to my identity drop away. I feel good about who I was and about who I am. Now I see a lovable child, who happened to be a victim of others' unhappiness.

Today I will choose to see my past through different eyes and in so doing, will see myself anew.

I commend my love of learning.

Some days my inner child is a genius certain to win a Nobel Prize for physics. Other days the child says, "I will never learn long division and you are a Godzilla to make me learn it!"

Even as unpleasant as frustration feels when I am trying to master a new skill, I commend my love of learning. I heed my frustration as a valuable clue to how I learn best:

I may need to take a break. I may want to call a friend and moan and groan loudly. I may need to ask for help. Or perhaps I may need to let go of my perfectionism.

I know that frustration is an important part of learning and as all feelings do, it passes. Yet my mastery and competence stay with me. Today I will applaud my growing pains.

I can make good decisions.

In the past, I put decisions "on hold," letting them pile up for fear of making mistakes. Often I made decisions by default. Making no choice is really making a choice.

Today I will make decisions based on what I know now. I will not let impulsiveness rule me or be pressured into making a decision before I am ready. Nor will I procrastinate to avoid making a mistake.

Rather, I will decide at my own pace with deliberation and in good faith. Mistakes are allowed and I'm allowed to learn from them.

I cannot live without making decisions. Knowing this, I will make decisions confidently and without fear. Trusting my decisions, I will do the best I can today.

Today I discover my strengths my way.

Children want to do things their way. They are mastering skills and discovering their own unique method of learning.

Some children learn best through pictures and words, while some collect information best through listening. Others need hands-on experience, using their bodies to store information.

When children are allowed to learn their way, they discover their own strengths. As a child growing up in a dysfunctional family, I did not learn about my unique strengths. I thought there was only one way to study or work or play.

As an adult in recovery, I am discovering both my way and new ways. My strengths are my foundation for learning. Today I will choose one activity and do it *MY WAY.*

Vulnerability is a part of my humanness.

When I was a child, I was certain that adults knew something I didn't know, something that made life perfectly clear. I thought that adults were in control of this secret, and that when I grew up, this secret would also be revealed to me.

I couldn't wait to grow up and learn this secret. Yet when I became an adult, I still felt as confused and vulnerable as I did when I was a child. What was this secret that no one would tell me?

Now I know the secret: Grown-ups are often as scared and vulnerable and in need of help as children. We don't know everything, we're not always in control. And that's okay.

Today I will share this simple truth with others to dispel their despair. Vulnerability knows no age limit, it is a part of our humanness.

Today I will welcome my limits.

Today I will set some limits in my life. Just because my family lived in chaos doesn't mean I have to.

I once rebelled against the very idea of limits. To me, they seemed like the walls of a prison. Now I see that far from imprisoning me, limits give me a framework within which I am free and safe to explore.

Without being held in the confines of its banks, a river could not flow to the sea. Without limits, life is chaos.

Today I will welcome my limits. They free me to be me.

My inner child is a wonderful part of me.

The child inside me is afraid and she doesn't quite know why. My inner child wants to curl up in a ball and leave the living to those who know how to grow up and be successful at it.

My child inside peers through a crack to see what everyone else does and then tries to mimic what she sees. Yet when she mimics, she doesn't always get it quite right.

Today I will cuddle my child within. I will encourage her to let go of at least one fear. I will take her for a ride and together we will throw the fear out of the window and wave goodbye to it.

Today I will encourage my inner child to be who she was created to be. If she is a quiet child, that's okay. If she is a playful child, that's okay, too. Today I will let my inner child know I'm glad she is alive and a wonderful part of me.

I can let go of the burden of managing the world.

Life in my dysfunctional family was totally out of control and unpredictable. The chaos left me deeply scarred. In pain, I resolved to gain control over my life and over whoever and whatever might affect me in some way.

As I have grown toward health, I have been able to reassure the hurt child within me that I am now wise enough and powerful enough to take care of him. He no longer needs to live in fear of life being out of control, for I have discovered a wellspring of happiness within myself that is not dependent on others. I can take responsibility for creating a satisfying life of my own.

Today I will release my need to control others. I will walk free of the tremendous burden of having to manage the world. `

**I possess the courage to choose
the direction of my life.**

I can live the kind of life that the deepest part of me desires. I have the courage to make decisions which will enhance my life, and I have a willingness and determination to act on my decisions.

I am on a voyage of discovery. I am discovering the core issues that prevent me from enjoying life. I am discovering the specific fears that inhibit the growth of my full potential. I am discovering my motivations and intentions so that I can make clear decisions.

All of my discoveries — everything that I learn — help me to take full responsibility and help me create new and positive paths to follow.

Today I am inspired to search within for the strength to continue to freely choose the direction of my life.

I take satisfaction in change today.

I am aware of change in myself and I rejoice in it. With my inner child alive within me, I am ecstatically alive and attuned to the world around me.

Autumn brings a ripening, a time of fruition. Autumn is mine to harvest all the bounty of good that surrounds me. Leaves turn color and drift to the ground. I too go through changes, changes of growth.

My soul and spirit are keenly attuned to the tug and nip of autumn. I sense the artistry of a Higher Power in the evolution of all living things. I am an integral part of nature, as unique and perfect as everything that surrounds me.

I rejoice in my recovery, revel in my changes and growth that allow me to feel at home once again with nature.

Mistakes are an opportunity for growth.

When I was young, I thought that when I made a mistake, I must be really stupid. I always seemed to be screwing up, and my parents and siblings and even my friends let me know it. Gradually, I came to believe that I couldn't do anything right.

Today I will help my inner child learn that a mistake is an opportunity for growth. Each mistake says, "Here's an area that needs work." It is not a reflection of my self-worth. Making mistakes is not the issue; not learning from my mistakes is.

So today if I make a mistake on a drawing, I will use it as the basis for a different drawing. If I make a mistake in a friendship, I will treat it as an opportunity to change my behavior and make the friendship stronger. I welcome mistakes that give me the chance to grow.

My ethical standards reflect
my inner goodness.

I discover my ethical standards within my unfolding sense of self. As I grow in recovery, my self-respect allows me to respond respectfully to others.

In dysfunctional families, healthy morals are taught in an unhealthy way. Parents who are rigid and shaming have unreasonable expectations about their children's capacity to understand ethical behavior.

Like any other skill, moral understanding and ethical behavior grow in developmental cycles. When I was a child, my parents judged my behavior by adult standards. I felt shame rather than appropriate guilt when my actions fell short.

Today I will take stock of my moral values and ethical standards to make certain they reflect my inner goodness.

**I will allow my inner child
to wish and dream.**

Wishing won't make it happen but wishing brings me closer to my dream. It creates the fertile bed in which my dreams can grow. Wishing opens my heart to possibilities. It directs my soul and my heart and gives me hope for the future.

Wishing used to be a thing of childhood: wishing on a star, wishing before blowing out birthday candles, wishing in the night when awful noises rattled through the house.

This week I will let my inner child make her wishes. I will let her wish on stars, candles and just because. I will applaud her wishes and let them reside without ridicule in my heart. And someday maybe I will see those wishes become realities. If they don't, the wishes themselves will bring happiness and direction to my life.

I am powerful and I have needs.

As my inner child grows more powerful, I become more skilled at meeting my needs. One of the tasks in growing up is to learn to ask for help directly.

In my dysfunctional family, I felt torn between my desire for independence and my neediness. If I asserted my power, I lost my right to have needs. If I asked for help, I lost my hard-won power.

Today I will accept that my personal power and my needs are inseparable. If I give up my personal power, I am vulnerable to victimization or abuse. If I give up my needs, I become hard, angry and rigid.

In recovery, I strive for a balance of strength *and* vulnerability. This balance will come when I recognize my own needs and respond to them powerfully.

I restore my health with beauty.

In my healing, I feel the same deep sense of beauty that I feel when listening to powerful music or gazing at a magnificent mountain.

In Navaho healing ceremonies, illness is cured with paintings created from colored sand. Sandstone is ground and mixed with cornmeal, flowers, pollen and parts of plants to create colors of red, yellow, white and gray-blue. The colored sand is meticulously sifted into geometric patterns, each one designed for a specific ailment.

During the ceremony, the patient sits on the painting. The illness is absorbed into the intricate geometric design. Health is restored through beauty.

Today I will acknowledge my healing as a work of art. When I restore my health with beauty, beauty is restored about me.

Each day I grow more confident.

At the playground I watch a four-year-old work and work and work to climb the fire pole. She focuses all her intensity on her task and when inevitably she slips down, she tries again. I am amazed at her efforts. When I was four years old, I was easily frustrated. If I didn't succeed on the first try, I got angry. Unfortunately my anger wasn't allowed. So I turned my anger inward and learned to give up.

Today I will allow the four-year-old within me to work at climbing the pole. She grasps the pole with her hands and wraps her legs around it, pulling herself up. Then she slips because her muscles aren't strong enough. She wants to quit but I tell her what a great first attempt she made. Encouraged, she tries again.

One day she climbs all the way to the top! Then she gets her reward: a glorious slide to the ground and the chance to climb again.

Today I will allow my partner to be human.

Because my parents were never there for me emotionally, I grew up with an insatiable desire for love and acceptance. My need led me to create an image of a person who could meet all my emotional needs.

Unfortunately, my myth of the perfect partner has soured my intimate relationships. Because of it I have neglected the task of taking responsibility for my own happiness.

Today I will allow my partner to be human. This does not mean I will submit to an abusive relationship. Giving my partner the freedom to be less than perfect is different than giving him or her the freedom to abuse me.

Today I will freely release my partner from the burden of meeting all of my emotional needs.

My intuition is grounded in reality.

I trust my intuition and honor its place in my decision making.

I do not have to understand all that my intuition picks up with its finely tuned antenna. My intuition may direct my senses to observe minute details. Someone may sound good and say the right thing but my intuition collects other data. Body language and tone of voice may elicit painful memories and my intuition is the first to respond with alarm.

I did not trust my intuition growing up in a dysfunctional family. Reality was denied in countless ways and I received no validation for my inner voice that spoke the truth.

Today I will accept that my intuition is grounded in reality. I will consult that valuable part of myself and listen to its sage advice as I make decisions.

**Today and every day I will
affirm my growth.**

"You're stupid . . . You're ugly . . . Why did you have to be born?"

My inner child shouts these words whenever I am about to succeed, whenever I'm about to think something nice about myself. After hearing them so often, my inner child believes these words are true.

From this day forward, these words will not be part of my self-talk. Instead I will cuddle my inner child and tell her how worthy she is.

I will use new words to affirm me: "You did a good job . . . I can tell you did the best you could in that situation and I'm proud of you . . . I'm glad you were born."

Today and every day to come I will celebrate my growth. Today is exactly as it should be and I appreciate my progress.

I delight in all that I am.

Sometimes I stand before a mirror. I twist my neck to find new angles that reveal other facets of myself. My inner child sees a glamorous rock star, a foolish clown, a tough biker. I am rich, I am funny, I am powerful.

In my family of origin, co-dependency kept me stuck in rigid roles. I feared my family would abandon me if I experimented with different behaviors.

Today I will delight in all that I can be and all that I am. I may explore new roles and ways of being. I may choose a hairstyle or buy a trendy outfit. I may seek out new places and open myself to new friendships. And with each new adventure I will give my inner child something to celebrate.

I am the loving parent to my inner child.

A newborn infant is wrapped in warm towels and placed in his mother's outstretched arms. Mother is wet with the perspiration of giving birth. Her face is wet with tears of wonder and love. Gently she unwraps her baby and counts his fingers and toes. She closely examines her child's body and welcomes him into this new life.

He begins to cry. Without hesitation his mother offers her breast to him, giving him sustenance.

As an adult, I am the parent to the infant inside who sometimes needs sustenance to go on and face life. With loving care and guidance I can provide my infant with whatever he needs to build a solid foundation for life. When my infant within cries, I, too, feel hurt or vulnerable and need to be cuddled, fed or softly reassured. I will take responsibility for myself and my child today.

Today I choose to love myself more.

Tonight I feel the shame that I always feel when I have given in to addictive behavior. The lack of unconditional love in my dysfunctional family created an aching void inside me. Because I did not know how to fill this void in a healthy way, I covered my pain with self-destructive behavior. Although I'm not responsible for the forces that have brought me to this place, I am responsible for what I do with my life from now on. I know that my addictions rob me of the self-esteem that is the foundation of my journey toward wholeness.

Today I will reaffirm my commitment to fill my life with only life-giving activities. If faced with the choice of overindulgence, overwork or over-dependency, I will first ask myself, "Will I love myself more, or less, if I engage in this activity?"

Today I choose to love myself more.

Today I envision a healthy future.

Today I will refuse to play the tapes from the past filled with their critical messages. Instead, I will envision myself as I will be. The seeds of my future healthy self have already taken root within me. I see the child within me emerging from fear into confidence and peace.

I see myself laughing and loving, full of life and attracting only life-giving relationships. I feel the deep satisfaction that will come by setting and maintaining personal boundaries. I sense the warm glow of healthy self-esteem within me as I learn to nurture and take care of myself.

I know without a doubt that I am the person in my vision, experiencing all the joys of a full and satisfying life. The damage of the past is behind me. Today I will nurture the seeds of life and health that are growing day by day.

Today I will place all my concerns into the hands of my Higher Power.

In the still of the night, jumbled thoughts race through my mind. Their frantic activity keeps me from healing sleep. Each problem from the day is considered and reconsidered. Each hurt is felt again. Memories return to me from childhood, when bedtime was anxiety-provoking and frightening.

Tonight I will entrust all my concerns from the day to the strong hands of my Higher Power. I will have faith that I can review them with fresh eyes tomorrow morning.

It is not necessary to solve all my problems tonight or even within the next week. Some things are best taken care of slowly, over time. I will reassure my inner child that resolution comes one day at a time.

I don't have to be quiet to be good.

I learned early to equate being quiet with being good: "She's so good, she never complains." "What a good baby, she never cries." "Don't discuss family business outside the family."

No one in my family was allowed to complain because nothing could ever be wrong. If one thing was wrong that might mean everything was wrong. And that simply wouldn't do, for my family was deeply invested in maintaining the appearance of normality.

After a while I didn't believe my own eyes and ears. If a situation seemed not quite right, my perception must be wrong. So I just kept quiet about everything.

Today I will allow my inner child to complain about an unfair situation. I hear her complaint and I listen carefully. I can trust my inner child's perception of reality.

Tonight I will calm my terrorized inner child.

Growing up in my family often felt like Halloween. I never knew when my parents would treat us to nurturing and affection or trick us with their abuse. The mask of addiction pervaded my home and I lived in fearful anticipation of what life would bring. Now I must face the ghost of the terrorized child that haunts me. This frightened little girl hates surprises and remains on mental alert to guard against harm.

Tonight is Halloween. When my inner child knocks at the door of my consciousness, I will open it and greet her with a smile. I will tell her to reach into the treat bag as deeply as she can, to take as much as she needs and to come back as often as she wants. Together we will learn to be treated, not tricked.

I am learning to anticipate the pleasant surprises that life holds in store. I know that I can handle the ghosts and goblins of my painful childhood should they appear on my doorstep.

I can maintain friendships.

Healthy relationships support recovery and I choose friends who delight in my growth.

During my childhood, my parents never tried to help maintain bonds of friendship. I rarely felt comfortable inviting friends home and I often felt isolated.

As an adult child, I have changed jobs and said goodbye forever to former colleagues. I denied my feelings of loss and, in so doing, denied my need to stay bonded. I did not learn that friendships can change and still remain vital.

Today I stay connected in friendships that I want to maintain. I move forward with confidence, trusting that my growth will strengthen my relationships.

Today I will learn to accept nurturing touch.

Sometimes I'm afraid to accept touch. I fear my own passions will suddenly take on a life of their own, pulling me into situations for which I am not prepared. I am also afraid of touch because I am so touch-starved — hungry for that which I deserved but rarely, if ever, received.

Today I will begin learning how to accept touch by telling one close friend about my needs and my fears. Perhaps I will ask for a short hug whenever we meet or a touch on my arm while we talk. When touch becomes scary, I will allow myself to tell my friend that I need to back away until I feel comfortable again. It is okay not to let someone touch me without my permission. But I will learn to accept nurturing touches that will help me to grow in love for myself and others.

I am learning to take risks.

Today I will be fully alive as I dive headlong into life. I will not shrink from taking risks. For too long now my life has been characterized by a boredom born of routine. In seeking security, I have settled into a rut that has begun to look like a tomb. Today I want to explore and challenge my physical, mental and spiritual boundaries. I want to feel the exhilaration that comes from new experiences.

To succeed in breaking out of my rut, I know I'll need to reassure my inner child that I will take good care of her. I understand her strong need for safety but I also believe she deserves more from life. If I am to avoid a slow kind of dying in the years ahead, I must stretch my limits. I must conquer my fear of the new to forge a more satisfying life for myself.

Today I will let go of my need to control.

Life in my chaotic family was like living in a stagecoach pulled by a team of wild horses. I felt that if I didn't keep a tight rein on everything, we would all go tumbling over the edge into oblivion.

Having pulled back on the reins without letup for so many years, my hands don't know how to let go. I feel I have to control every aspect of life or I will be smashed to death on the rocks below.

Today I will begin to let go of the reins. As my fingers loosen, the reins drop slackly into my lap. No longer straining against the harsh pull of the bit, the horses begin to slow down and find their own way. They stop in a meadow and put their heads down to eat the sweet grass. I take the halters off their necks and they prance with joy at their freedom. I relax, enjoying my own freedom. As the sun sets, I harness the horses and start back down the path. I trust them to find their own way home.

I am open to giving and receiving.

Today I will not only affirm myself but those around me. Our spirit soars when we receive affirmation, it falters and plunges when we are abused by criticism.

Opening my eyes to those around me, I will go out of my way to make positive, true statements of respect and appreciation for those around me. Today I will call or write a note to three friends and let them know what I appreciate about them.

In my healing process, I sometimes become focused on my needs, forgetting those who touch my life and encourage me. When I see and comment on their honorable or noble aspects, I add to their sense of self-worth. In giving, I also enhance my own self-worth.

Today I am curious about everything I see.

Today I look at each thing I encounter as though I have never seen it before. I see the smallest detail in the petals of a tiny flower, in the swirls of food on a dirty dish, in the rippling sheets on my unmade bed. I allow my curiosity its freedom.

When I was younger, my parents and teachers and even other children belittled me for asking questions. "Everybody knows that," said the kids. "You ask too many questions," said the adults. So I stopped asking questions of others and then I stopped asking myself.

Today I ask, "Why?" And I listen for the answers.

Today I will trust my body.

Today I trust my body to be capable and strong. I am confident of its ability. Yet sometimes I still hear the voice that warns, "Careful, don't fall!" and "That's too high, come down now!"

When I was a child, my parents worried that I might hurt myself. They taught me to doubt that my body would do what I wanted it to do. I believed my arms and legs might let me down and so I was afraid of physical activity and unaware of the joy it brings.

Today I know that my body has its own wisdom and I allow it to find its own way. I wonder at the sheer joy of walking briskly, one sure step after another, as I explore a new path.

I am developing consistency in my life.

The ocean moves in a consistent rhythm. It rushes in with mighty force and retreats in gentleness.

Consistency was never a part of my home during my growing years. Thus, as an adult, I have viewed consistency as boring, preferring to add unnecessary drama to my life. As I look back on this chaos, I realize that accountability and consistency are qualities that will add to my comfort and security.

Today I will choose to be like the ocean, consistent in my actions, powerful but gentle. It is within my power to be consistent. Making goals and flexible plans to reach them will help me develop this quality. I will benefit by enlisting the help of trusted friends who will encourage me in this endeavor.

I am a safe haven for my inner child.

My inner child is running scared. She's not yet old enough or strong enough or wise enough in the ways of the world. She does not yet know how to take care of herself.

I am a safe haven for my inner child. I envelop her with my warm body, loving arms and soft words. I am the place she can stay for as long as she needs to. When she feels safe enough, she can show herself to the world again. I protect her from those things she's not yet ready to confront and I encourage her to do the things I know she can do. When she feels she has no place to turn, she can turn to me. I am "home" to my inner child.

Today I will play.

Every time I went to a toy store, I always heard my parents' voice saying "Don't touch that. Put that down. *No*, you cannot have this toy." Today I will take my inner child to a toy store and play with any toy I fancy.

In kaleidoscopes: I see colors and shapes in endless patterns. Plastic beads, wooden beads, sequins and sparkles to adorn my wrists and fingers.

Among the stuffed teddy bears and rubber ducks I choose the animal of my dreams. Drums and cymbals, whistles and noisemakers beat out rhythms and make shrill noises.

If I want, I may buy a toy for my inner child. Or we may go home and make a toy of cardboard boxes, pillows or water-filled bottles. Today I will find a toy and play.

Today I discern between fantasy and reality.

As a child, I tried to understand the difference between fantasy and reality. Unfortunately, my parents were addicted and could not help me. I can still feel the terror that stemmed from my belief that I was the cause of awful events! Was I really bad enough to cause Mom's drinking? Did I cause my dad to get sick? Deep within I have a three-year-old who questions cause and effect. As I let this child surface, I can visualize that little face with eyes filled with shame and confusion.

Today I will use my adult self to alleviate the anxiety that has plagued me and clear up my three-year-old's misconceptions. I will remind myself that children are at the mercy of the adults around them. A sense of well-being pervades my consciousness today as I replace magical thinking with a healthy reality.

I am learning to think before I act.

I am learning to think before I commit my time and energy to activities and requests from others. I give myself time to think through possibilities and consequences.

I can ask questions. I can decide yes or no, and I can see options between the two. I am learning to negotiate for what I want.

I still monitor my impulses and pay attention to my feelings but now I think before I act.

My reasoning is sound and valid. Whatever I decide is right for me at the time, and I can learn from my mistakes.

I create choices for myself when I think. Today I will think for myself and make decisions that are in my own best interest.

I give up my need for approval.

Today I will give up my excessive need for approval. In the controlling, co-dependent environment of my childhood home, my safety depended on pleasing my parents. I learned to watch for the smallest signs of disapproval from them to tell me how to behave. As a result, I still feel the presence of a frightened little boy within me drives me to say and do things that will earn favor with others.

I will no longer allow my excessive need for approval to rob me of inner peace. I visualize the frightened five-year-old inside me bathed in a pool of warm light. I feel his fear dissolving in the security of my love for him.

A feeling of peace wells up in me as my fear of disapproval melts away. I step forward confidently to face the new day.

I am learning to let go.

When I was five years old, I loved to watch balloons float higher and higher and higher into the sky, until they disappeared behind the sun. I imagined they had gone somewhere I had never been.

Today I will release my own balloons. With the help of my inner child, I will put each of my fears into its own balloon. Then I'll say good-bye and let it go. I may feel sad at their leaving because I have grown used to my fears, but I will also feel happy, because now there is room for my hopes and my dreams.

Again I will gather in my mind as many colorful balloons as I need, and into each I will put a hope and a dream. Joyfully I will release each one with the blessing that it take all the time it needs on its journey to grow and develop. I know that sometime I will find each balloon waiting for me along my path.

**Today I will set safe, reasonable
boundaries for myself.**

Boundaries are not limitations. They map out
my comfort zone from which I can soar in the
freedom of who I am. Because I care about me
and want the best for this person who is valuable, I will create my own boundaries. Carefully
constructed, they will reflect where I am in my
own emotional growth.

Sometimes others may not like the boundaries
I set. I will maintain the boundaries in spite of
their wishes and desires. I must feel safe to
grow fully.

Boundaries are not cement barriers. They can
be moved to accommodate new growth. I
choose to give myself a safe place to grow by
setting boundaries so others cannot intrude. It
is a loving thing to do to set my limits.

I can choose qualities that enhance my life.

You can't rush a fine portrait. If you do, the colors run together in shades of brown and gray. An oil painting must be worked on a little at a time, allowing the colors to dry between sittings.

Sometimes the artist will even work on another painting for a time. Indeed the experience gained in doing the second painting only enhances the skill of the artist and, therefore, the value of the portrait.

My life is a fine portrait, worthy of the best materials I can put into it. It is worth taking time. Sometimes I rush because I want the portrait finished *now*. Today I will take one step at a time, not rushing, not holding back. I will choose those "paints" that will make my portrait the best it can be — the best relationships, the best choices, the best affirmations.

I am fully alive when I feel
and express my emotions.

I sense today the stirring of feelings once frozen deep inside me.

In my dysfunctional family, hope was ridiculed, joy was minimized, love was manipulated and anger was met with violence. As a result, I kept my feelings a secret from my family and even from myself.

Now, as an adult, I am afraid to let myself hope and love because these feelings leave me vulnerable to the pain of broken dreams and promises. I seldom let myself feel anger and fear because these feelings seem to overwhelm the little child within me.

Today I will release my feelings from their icy prison within. I will also reassure my inner child that I can handle my feelings so no harm can come to us. I choose today to be fully alive by accepting and experiencing the full range of my emotions.

I will open my ears to healing sounds.

Thump thump dump. Boo hoo shoes. Rick rack rock. Children love the sounds of rhyme and rhythm in language. Many children's songs and games are simple chants that put words together for the pure pleasure of sound.

Playful sounds attract children to language and build a foundation for reading and writing. However, in my family, words sounded harsh and caused emotional pain. As a child, I blocked out many sounds to protect myself from pain. As an adult child, I still blank out certain words during conversations.

Today I will invite my inner child to listen to playful sounds. I may read aloud from a book of poetry; I may sing aloud in the car or in the shower because the sounds feel good. I may phone a trusted friend and ask to hear words of affirmation. Today I will open my ears to healing sounds.

I can be grown-up and still be loved.

Love was a conditional commodity in my dysfunctional family. Love was doled out as a reward for pleasing my parents. It was withdrawn as a punishment for displeasing them. I soon became convinced that I could be loved only if I was dependent and accommodating.

Because my parents' love was conditional, my inner child and I confuse pleasing with love. When those close to me disagree with me or are angry with me, I feel certain they don't love me anymore. As a result, I seldom express a difference of opinion with others, for fear that they will withdraw their love as my parents did.

The time has come for me to undo this destructive conditioning. Not everyone is as limited in their ability to love as my parents were. No longer do I assume that others will abandon me when they get angry with me. I *can* think and act independently and not fear rejection. I can act grown-up and still be loved.

Tonight I will love my inner child to sleep.

Tonight as my head rests on my pillow, I want to let go of the affairs of today. Yet my mind is so busy and my body so tight that I cannot relax.

Memories of a child listening to screaming arguments flood my mind. I see a little boy who lay in bed churning thoughts over and over in a desperate attempt to make sense of the craziness. The five-year-old inside me remains on mental alert so he will not be harmed.

This evening when I go to bed I will cradle my inner child in my thoughts. I will surround him with a white protective light and provide him with the safety that he so desperately craves and needs. I will speak to him with a gentle voice filled with love and reassurance. A feeling of peace begins to permeate my body and my mind. My mind is calm and deeply still as I love my inner child to sleep.

I can do things for myself.

When I was about three years old, I had already learned to get others to do things for me by being weak and helpless. If I just whined and sniffled long enough, someone would get my toy for me, bring me a cookie or lift me up and carry me wherever I wanted to go.

Even after I had grown up, this dependent behavior still worked really well. When things went wrong, I cried to get someone's sympathy and assistance instead of learning to solve my own problems. After years of this, I came to believe that I really was helpless.

Today I will teach the three-year-old within me to use her own strength. Instead of crying and complaining when things don't go my way, I'll try to find out what's wrong and explore ways to make it right. I can do things for myself.

My rules support my recovery.

A child questions rules. If a brother or a sister is allowed to stay up later than usual, the child asks, "Why can't I?" In a healthy family, parents welcome the child's questions as a teaching opportunity. The brother or sister may be older or celebrating a special occasion. Children may not like certain rules but these rules provide security. When allowed to question, a child grows in reasoning power and develops self-discipline.

My inner child questions the rules that I have chosen for my recovery. As I grow I am learning to structure rules based on self-respect.

Today I welcome my inner child's questions as a learning opportunity. I will choose and adhere to rules that support my growth.

I am entitled to harvest all that I desire from life.

At this fall season, I think of harvest time. I have worked strenuously throughout the year and it is time to gather in some of the good that I have sown. Just as there has been a seed sown for every stalk of corn, so for every good effect, there was first a cause. In order to enjoy my harvest, I have had to plant healthy ideas followed by positive actions.

At this harvest time, if I am returning home from the fields with an "empty basket," perhaps I haven't given my recovery the importance it deserves. If I want to count on a consistent supply of the abundance life has to offer, I must plant and tend to my own crop. Am I busily running about engaged in endless activity? Or am I fully conscious of my patterns and actively involved in trying to change them? I am deserving of an overflowing harvest. Today I will consciously plant those thoughts that will help me achieve what I desire.

It's okay for me to ask for help.

It is embarrassing and shameful to let others know I have needs. As a youngster, I got the message to hurry and grow up. I learned that asking for help brought either disaster or disappointment. It is important for me to learn to ask for the care I need, to know that caring for myself is sometimes a task that is too large for just one person.

Sometimes I need help to make it through. Sometimes I need the physical strength of one, the electronic know-how of another, the legal or medical advice of yet another. Sometimes I need a hug or a listening ear.

Others are willing to give . . . If I will only ask.

I am discovering the essence of who I am.

I sense a stirring with me today. Freed from the trauma of the past, my essence is eager to emerge. My child within, who has long been dormant, is thawing to life in the environment of love with which I have surrounded myself.

Survival was the focus of my early years, survival from emotional and physical abuse. To protect myself, I buried my true identity beneath a rigidly dictated role.

As an adult, my true self remained submerged until my facade began to crack and come apart. Although the crumbling of my facade is painful, the pain is mixed with joy as the real me emerges.

Today I will say yes to the stirring within me. I will fully explore what it means to be the wonderful, unique person I was created to be.

Today I honor the seasons of the self.

Today I welcome the necessary cycles of reparenting my inner child. There are times I feel like an infant and want to be nurtured. At times I feel defiant and stubborn like a testy two-year-old. When my adolescent feelings surface, I feel a surge of sexual energy along with a fiery rebellion. Healing comes when I can honor my inner child at whatever age and stage she presents herself to me.

Sometimes I feel stuck or impatient with my recovery process. I do not want to feel old feelings or work through old issues. Yet I am wiser than I was when I began my recovery and my maturity allows me to reach deeper levels of understanding. I choose to silence the critical inner voices of doubt and impatience.

Today I bring fresh experiences to old issues and recurring memories. Today I honor the seasons of the self.

I will listen carefully to my inner voice.

Growing up, I heard voices telling me who I was and what I would become. Most of the messages were negative and have soured my life.

Listening to those voices will no longer be an option for me. Today I will tune them out. Instead, I will listen to the small voice inside me struggling to be heard. This voice knows the truth of who I am and what I am capable of becoming.

In the past I had to listen to negative voices because there were no others. Today a positive chorus surrounds me. I will hear only the voices of those who accept me, encourage me and tell me the truth about who I am now. Above all I will listen carefully to that small inner voice struggling to be heard.

**Today I will create playful friendships
for my inner child.**

Today I will find a playmate for my inner child. Close friends support and enjoy each other but playmates can be casual friends or strangers. Children swing side by side with unfamiliar children on the playground. Perhaps a child's laugh or bright sweater attracts another child. They may seek each other out and run to play on the monkey bars or the seesaw together.

Adults who are strangers can also enjoy each other. They can share a joke at the bus stop or sweat together during an exercise class. Sometimes a friendship develops and it may or may not deepen. Nonetheless, the bonds of fun may last for years. I can phone a casual friend and share a laugh or get together for a fun outing.

Today I will welcome opportunities to create playful friendships. Today I will find a playmate.

Today I will allow myself to be.

Time has no meaning to infants. Clocks and schedules mean nothing. Infants sleep when they are sleepy. They wake when they are uncomfortable or rested or needy. They eat when they are hungry.

Removing my watch, I will allow myself to make my own schedule for one day. I will find a single day when I can just *be*. For a certain period, I will rest. For another, I will be. For another, I will eat. My needs will dictate my actions on this day.

I will nurture my inner infant in the ways it enjoys. If he needs to rock, I will rock him. If he needs to suck, I will have a juice bar or a piece of hard candy to fulfill his need. It feels good to take care of my infant.

At the end of the day, I will wrap myself tightly in a blanket and think how wonderful it is to be who I am.

I will meet the needs of
the child within — now.

Ever since childhood, I have lived by the principle of work now and play later. There was little lightheartedness or fun in my dysfunctional family. Pain was the dominant experience. Pleasure was always something to be experienced later, when the current trauma had passed.

Well, "later" never seemed to come and I grew to adulthood with a distorted view of life. I believed that the present is for working and taking care of problems and the future is for pleasure . . . maybe.

Yet it's not too late to help my inner child learn to play. Indeed, if I am to recover, I must learn to balance work and pleasure.

Today I will take time for lighthearted joy as well as for work.

I embrace the ideal of a loving God.

At times I find it difficult to embrace the notion of a God who loves me unconditionally. I know that an integral part of recovery is the development of a healthy spiritual base. Even now, I am aware of an everpresent doubt that lurks in my soul. How could God love a mistake? How could such a precious child be so viciously punished? Growing up in a dysfunctional family left me spiritually bankrupt. Unfortunately I filled this void with destructive ideas based on the perceptions of a frightened child. When I made mistakes, my parents punished me by saying I was bad, threatening that God would punish me. No wonder thoughts of a Higher Power provide so little comfort now.

Today I will cradle my frightened inner child in my lap. I will speak about ideas of faith, expectations of good and the realization of plenty.

I allow my anger to have a voice.

Living in my dysfunctional home was like sailing a boat through a hurricane. I lived in fear of being capsized by sudden outbursts and unpredictable rages. "Don't yell at me!" one or the other of my parents would shout. "I'm the adult, you're the child! Go to your room."

I received plenty of anger but I could not express my own. I was terrified of the anger of others. I tried to keep my world calm.

Because I have not learned to express my own anger, it comes out sideways. It whines. It masks itself with false sweetness. Sometimes my anger is hidden even from me and I become depressed.

Today I will permit my inner child to express anger. When I allow my anger to speak with its own voice, it delivers its message succinctly and waits for an answer. I am not afraid of my anger.

**Today I will enjoy the pleasure
of self-discipline.**

In winter, the tree outside my window is
bare. Branches grow out of its trunk. Each
branch supports the twigs from which the
leaves will sprout. Its ordered growth is a
model for my own.

As part of my recovery, I am learning to
support my growth by establishing healthy
rules and order. I base my self-discipline on
self-esteem rather than on fear of abandonment or punishment.

As a child, I lived in chaos. Some rules were
rigid, others were nonexistent. Hungry or not, I
learned to clean my plate but I did not learn
rules for a proper diet. I learned to be polite but
I did not learn rules for developing relationships.

Today I will enjoy the pleasure afforded by my
self-discipline. I will adhere to appropriate rules
that bring order to my recovery.

I let go of the past and embrace my new freedom.

The steam engine chugs down the track, moving the train forward, leaving the past behind. As I sit in one of the passenger seats, I look out of the window, thinking about what has been left behind. Some thoughts remind me of the baggage cluttered around my feet. It's difficult to travel through life with all this baggage. It's time to lighten my load by getting rid of the things I no longer need.

Moving to the rear of the train, I struggle with a bag stuffed with attitudes from my family of origin. I struggle with my need to take care of everyone I meet and my willingness to manipulate others. I stand in the caboose and lift the bag high enough to clear the railing. With a mighty heave, I throw the bag off the train and I am free.

Today I will call upon my adult self to clear out useless baggage.

Today I learn to please my inner child.

My inner child loves to explore new ways of being: Imagine living in another country in another time. Imagine becoming the fine mist rising from the rocks below a waterfall.

When I was a child, my parents did not accept the new ways of being that I explored. So I learned to think and behave in ways that narrowed my sense of self.

In recovery, I am discovering parts of myself that surprise me, sometimes with delight and sometimes with fear. I can explore because of the safe grounded place inside me.

Today I will pretend with my inner child. I may imagine myself to be another person or an object. I may make animal sounds or machine sounds. I may feel strange or silly, whatever pleases the child within me.

I will discover the art of stillness.

The child sits watching the clouds drift lazily by. His mother calls, "Do something. You mustn't waste time."

In our culture, activity is thought to be good and the lack of it bad. So we race around and fill our lives with one activity after another and get nowhere. We forget the little child within who needs to sit and contemplate clouds or stars or a spider spinning its web. We forget the inner child who needs to pet a horse or play with a dog. This child is not lazy. Indeed, by doing these things, this child learns about life and rest and needs and play and balance.

This week I will set aside time to do nothing. Perhaps I will choose activities that I consider "lazy" and therefore never do. I will discover that energy comes from sitting still and from the art of being.

I choose what is right for me today.

Today I see the range of choices in my life. I do not have to choose between black and white; I may choose red or gold. I do not always have to choose between right and wrong; I may choose the best for me at the time.

Dysfunctional families make choices from fear. To minimize the feelings of fear and inadequacy, parents in these families structure all choices as right and wrong. I grew up without choices. There is no free choice when all alternatives are punishing; true alternatives are positive possibilities.

Today I will see choices as possibilities. I will explore a range of options and then choose. The choices I consider today give me possibilities for tomorrow.

I will face my anger today.

Children fight and bicker over rules and toys and boundaries. They attempt to manipulate each other with promises and threats. In the end, who wins?

They all do, because with every fight they learn important lessons about other people and themselves. They learn when to compromise and when to stick to what is important to them. Also they learn when to say, "No! I won't! And you can't make me!" These words come in quite handy in my adult life.

In my family, it was dangerous to express anger. As a result, I often run from conflict. Today I will face what might hurt. For I know that in the end I will learn. And learning means winning the war, even though I may lose a battle.

Today I will use my two-year-old energy to speak up for myself.

**I grow in competency and I measure
my skills against realistic standards.**

I measure my competence against realistic and
objective standards. I do not judge my self-
worth; I do not expect perfection. I am learning
to master new skills, and standards are merely
a measure to aid my growth.

As an adult child, I judged my efforts harshly. I
avoided objective comments about my work
performance and my social interactions. Many
times I failed to hear praise and admiration. I
based my self-worth on the approval of others.

As an adult in recovery, I can let go of perfectionism. I can seek out and hear objective feedback
and I can agree or disagree with another's opinion. As I observe others' behavior and performance, I can accept or reject their standards.

Today I will judge my skills realistically and
acknowledge my successes as well as my
mistakes.

**The child within me is playful,
beautiful and expressive.**

There is a child within me who needs love and
attention. It is this precious child that knows
how to play and accept love. It is this precious
child that I am discovering.

Today I open my heart to my inner child and
know that it still lives in me today. Throughout
the day, I will let the memories of my childhood
flow. Whether painful or pleasant, I know these
memories will help me discover an important
part of myself that I've ignored.

I will nurture the child within me with tender-
ness and warmth. As I love and accept the child
within me, I feel the wonderful playful part of
me emerge.

I am learning to care for myself.

When I was just learning to walk and run, I fell down a lot. When I burst into tears, grown-ups and children alike told me to stop being such a crybaby. So I learned not to cry. But I still hurt sometimes and no one was there to comfort me. I learned how to live with my pain but not how to make it go away.

Today I am learning to comfort myself. When I hurt, I let myself cry. I allow my tears to wash my pain away. I wrap my arms around myself and hug myself tightly. I hug a big plush pillow to me, burying my head in its squishy softness. I rock gently back and forth until all the pain and tension leave my body. I sit quietly for a moment, slowly inhaling and exhaling deep breaths.

A feeling of satisfaction begins to permeate my consciousness. I am learning how to care for myself.

I am responsible for myself.

As a child, I thought I was responsible for the adults in my world. Somehow, I felt responsible for the good things and bad things that happened to them.

I spoke, acted and even breathed in ways I hoped would make them happy. Sometimes it worked. Sometimes it didn't.

Today I understand and accept that I have no control over anyone's actions or emotions. Nor does anyone have control over mine. No longer will my childish attitude of "he made me" excuse me from being responsible for my own deeds.

My emotions are okay. The emotions of those around me are okay. I will affirm my own uniqueness and that of others.

Today I will let the universe lead me.

In my chaotic family, the house was always a wreck. I couldn't count on anyone. If I didn't take care of things, they didn't get done. I felt that if I didn't attend to every last detail, my life would go spinning out of control. I was afraid of what might happen to me in an unknown world.

Even though I am an adult now, my inner child still exerts a lot of effort trying to control every aspect of my life and I'm tired.

Today I will let the universe lead the way. I will be very quiet, let go of all my preconceived ideas, open all my senses and let life lead me. If I hear a voice calling, I will listen. If a new thought comes into my mind, I will welcome it as I would a new friend. My inner child can feel safe in the wisdom of the universe.

My recovery affirms life.

My goodness is the affirmation of life. I choose what is good for my recovery and I achieve goodness through the unfolding of my human potential.

My Higher Power affirms every part of creation, "And it is good." The goodness is more than beauty or excellence; the flower that grows from seed to bud to blossom is fulfilling the potential for which it was created.

As a part of nature, I fulfill my potential by living humanly. I fulfill my human potential by unfolding my individuality. I accept the creative force of my Higher Power within my life and I participate in my own creations through my recovery.

My recovery affirms life and I am good.

I am learning to trust my Higher Power.

Today I will seek to trust and receive the unconditional love of my Higher Power.

Yet there have been times when I have sensed a barrier keeping me from accepting God's unconditional love. This barrier stems from my childhood and my unhealthy parents. Their love was conditional. "I'll love you *if* . . ." never "I love you . . . *period.*"

As a result, I have had to teach the fearful child within me the meaning of love by lavishing her with the unconditional love she never received. Just as she accepts the healing touch of my love for her, so too, will I accept God's unconditional love for me. All the tension leaves my body and I feel at peace as God whispers, "Just as you love your little one, so too, do I love you."

Today I will greet my emotions
with acceptance.

A little girl sits quietly and listens to the different voices of the wind. Some are soft and soothing, some violent and angry. Some tell, some sing and some laugh. One may be more likable than another but they each have a special purpose. And, unless the wind is destructive, all of the voices are acceptable.

I have hushed the inner voices of my emotions most of my life. From now on, every time I hear the wind, I will remember that my emotions are okay and valid.

Today as I feel the rush of my emotions sweep through me, I will greet them with acceptance and remind myself that it is okay for them to be.

**I create a future of growth for myself
and my world.**

Often teenagers receive mixed messages from
adults. On the one hand they are constantly
reminded that they "are the future." On the
other hand, they are taught that "things stay the
same." Before they have even started their future, they are condemned to repeat the past.

As an adult child, I felt despair and hopeless-
ness over the continuing dysfunction in my
family. I generalized my family experience to
the world at large. I felt over-responsible for
solving all the world's problems or I denied
any social responsibility.

In recovery, I am learning that change is
possible. I observe myself, and others in recovery, heal and grow. By replacing despair
with hope, I can create a genuine future of
growth for myself and I can envision a healthy
future for my world.

I am patient with my process.

A writer spins a tale, one sentence at a time. Each new sentence builds upon the last to create paragraphs, then pages, then chapters and finally, a book.

Similarly, a child learns first to roll over, then crawl, then stand and finally walks one step at a time.

It is now within my power to rewrite my entire life today. My recovery process is slow, full of starts and stops. I begin moving in one direction only to change and move in another. Giving myself the freedom to begin, to fail, to change direction helps me create a healthier life.

Today I will write one sentence of my new story. I will applaud my efforts and be gentle with myself.

I take steps toward fulfilling my desire.

Today I celebrate the exuberant child within who pushes the limits of my growth. I feel impassioned and vitalized as I envision new possibilities for my life.

I release all doubts and obligations from my past. I feel the weight of old burdens lifted. My body is relaxed and I walk with a spring in my step.

I trust that my desires are the foundation of my freedom. Exercising my freedom may mean wearing something outrageous, breaking away from the crowd or speaking up at a meeting.

Today I will choose one desire and take one step toward fulfilling it.

**Today I will use my childlike imagination
to transform adversity.**

A pile of rocks sits in an otherwise vacant lot.
No one gives them a second thought. They are,
at the least, a nuisance to walkers taking short-
cuts and, at the most, a problem for the owner
when it comes time to clear the land and build.

Yet to the children who gather to play in the lot
the rocks are an immediate asset. Moved just
so, they can be the walls of a fort. Or moved
over here and stacked like this, they become
the walls of a corral for the imaginary horses.
Large flat ones become bases for a ball game.
Tiny ones are food for the doll taken on a stroll.
Pretty ones are pocketed for future admiration.

Today I will take the rocks in my life and build
something from them. I will use my childlike
imagination to use those rocks to enhance my
life, not hinder it.

I can be powerful and have needs.

Today I will walk the fine line between being powerful and having needs.

My wounded inner child wants to take refuge either in the rigid role of the tough guy who needs no one or in the dependent role of the powerless victim. Today I will love the frightened little one within me and reassure him that his needs will be met.

Today though it may be uncomfortable, I will hold both feelings in equilibrium. I am a powerful person, full of ability and potential but I am also a person with needs. Today without becoming dependent, I will be open to the ways in which others may be able to help me meet my needs. Likewise, I will hold on to my personal power without becoming unapproachable.

I am learning the skills that improve my life.

A young girl skips rope in the school yard, her braids bouncing up and down. She falters, stops and begins again. She sings a little cadence that helps her keep the rhythm. She falters again, shifts the rope and jumps some more.

So much of my life is new to me. So much of what I do and feel were not part of my childhood. And sometimes I falter. Today, if I falter, I will remember the little girl in the school yard — how she stops a moment, readjusts and begins again. Through patient repetition, she learns to improve her skill. My repetition of the new things I am learning will better the skills I need to live a healthy life.

As I learn to grow, I will sing cadences to myself using words of affirmation, "I can, I will, I choose and it's okay." Today I will be the best rope jumper in the school yard.

Today I will allow my tears to come.

Tears accumulate in some plain jar inside my chest. I know the jar is full but I can't empty it. My child inside tells me crying isn't what grown-ups do. It isn't appropriate to let people see the pain leak out, is it? Crying means weakness and we can't be weak, we must be strong.

Today I will let the tears come. I will accept that tears are a sign of pain. And it's really okay to hurt. Tears are a sign of healing. And I do want to heal.

If the tears are locked tightly inside the jar, maybe I will watch a sad movie to unlock it. Maybe I will read a sad story. Or perhaps I will allow myself to remember that awful day when . . .

I won't stop the tears. I will let them stop themselves. Cleansed and refreshed, I am ready to begin a new day.

I create a holiday season that is special.

As the sounds of the holiday season surround me, so does the dissonance of past memories — painful memories that make me wish the season would pass by without my knowledge, without my participation.

Today I will make plans so that this holiday season will be mine and special. I will decide what I would like this season to be. If I want to surround myself with those I love, I will plan get-togethers that suit my needs. If I want to be alone to contemplate the wonder of the season, I will make specific plans to enhance the wonder. I will ask my inner child for advice on how to make this season special.

I will not allow this holiday season to pass in indecision. I will choose what is best for me. I will rejoice in what makes me happy.

On this holiday, I contemplate my faith.

A newborn infant cannot see its mother or father, yet she trusts that they are there. This is the beginning of a child's formation of faith and spirituality. When parents cannot be present because of addiction or compulsive behavior, children have difficulty developing a solid belief in themselves, other people and the world around them.

Yet it is so important for me to believe in qualities that are intangible. In recovery, I need faith to know that life can be better, that I don't need to live in pain.

On this holiday, I contemplate the unseen wonders of the world. I marvel at the planets that revolve without colliding. I consider the unseen power of love that transforms life.

I will open myself to the possibility of faith in myself and my world.

I am creating a tradition of healthy fun.

In the past, adults handed down their culture to children through folk games. Everyone from the youngest to the oldest were welcome to participate. Children learned rules, rituals and traditions while they played with adults. They also saw adults having fun and acting silly.

Today adults and children share fewer group games. Children teach each other the folk games; adults play organized sports with other adults. Increasingly, children's games are supervised by adults and are unhealthily competitive.

Today I will rediscover a group game I played as a child. I will create a family tradition of healthy fun for my children and the child within me.

I provide my inner child with structure.

A pair of swallows returns every year to the cubbyhole in the eaves of my porch. They make thousands of trips to build a mud nest for the anticipated arrival of their young. They share in the foundations of their future.

In my family, it was hard to build a foundation for the future. Fear of past failures inhibited the energy needed to look forward.

Like the swallows that make many trips to make their nest, I will allow myself many attempts and learn to be patient. My inner child will learn structure as I build my foundation. I will consult trusted friends for their ideas. I will not be ashamed if I cannot do it all by myself. With care and persistence, I will build the foundation for my future, one block at a time.

I embrace my humanness.

I can free myself from perfectionism and learn from my mistakes. My inner child is a fearless student and knows that mistakes are a necessary part of learning. Mistakes lead to knowledge and knowledge leads to success.

If I make a mistake and acknowledge it, I am on the way to achieving my goals.

While growing up, I feared mistakes and took inappropriate responsibility for what went wrong in my family. I limited both my risks and my opportunities to explore.

Today I will free the child within me to explore and take chances. I will transform my failures into successes and join the human race.

I expand my definition of who I am.

Today I seek my own name, my true identity. I am more than a co-dependent, a child of an addict or an incest survivor. I don't need to identify myself solely by these labels. They will always be a part of my identity, but now it's time to search inside for more.

I will take time to contemplate my recovery from the beginning until today. I have given voice to my inner child and it has become whole and healthier. I have given birth to my own truth that has allowed me to wipe away the fog of distortion about my family, my relationships and my own behavior. I honor where I have been and delight in where I am going.

My identity broadens as it encompasses qualities like courage, strength, integrity, beauty and vulnerability. As I make peace with my history, my identity is not just tied to the tragedies of my past. I include the present and future as I expand my definition of who I am.

I am allowing myself to receive.

I am used to being self-sufficient, never relying on others to help me through a crisis. As a child, I often had to depend on myself rather than ask the help of parents who couldn't be there for me.

Yet friends who want to be part of my life surround me. New friends offer gifts they are able to provide. Established friends are ready to offer a listening ear and wise counsel based on what they know of me. So often I turn them down, afraid that I might take advantage, become dependent and disappointed; betrayed once again.

Today I will open myself to trust. I will seek out one new friend and one old friend and allow myself to accept an offer they have given. In doing so, I will learn to trust a small bit more. I will also be building an important network of friends.

I look forward to the new year.

I pause between the passing of the old year and the beginning of the new. My plans for making necessary changes have already been set in motion. Their fulfillment lies ahead.

On this New Year's Eve, I take this moment to rest and reflect. I feel myself moving in perfect balance and harmony. I feel my connection to the earth and the universe. I know now that I am firmly set on my path. Even if I should stray for a moment, I will always find my way back.

I look back on the past year and rejoice in both my mistakes and my achievements. They have taught me well. I look forward to the new year with fresh eyes. I breathe in the stillness before time begins.

INDEX

367

368

372

My Personal Affirmations

My Personal Affirmations

More Affirmation Books

DAILY AFFIRMATIONS: For Adult Children of Alcoholics
Rokelle Lerner

Affirmations are positive, powerful statements that will change the ways we think, feel and behave. *Daily Affirmations* has also been recorded on audiocassette, where author Lerner is joined by Dr. Joseph Cruse.

ISBN 0-932194-27-3 .... $ 6.95

Set of Six 90-Minute Tapes
ISBN 0-932194-49-4 .... $39.95

SAY YES TO LIFE: Daily Meditations for Recovery
Leo Booth

Say Yes To Life takes you through the year day by day looking for answers and sometimes discovering that there are none. Father Leo tells us, "For the recovering compulsive person God is too important to miss — may you find Him now."

ISBN 0-932194-46-X .... $ 6.95

TIME FOR JOY
Ruth Fishel

With delightful illustrations by Bonny Lowell, Ruth Fishel takes you gently through the year, affirming that wherever you are today is perfect and now is the *TIME FOR JOY!*

ISBN 0-932194-82-6 .... $6.95

Best Sellers From HCI

ISBN	TITLE	PRICE
1-55874-112-7	Adult Children of Alcoholics (Expanded)	$8.95
0-932194-54-0	Bradshaw On: The Family	$9.95
0-932194-26-5	Choicemaking	$9.95
1-55874-040-6	Perfect Daughters	$8.95
1-55874-105-4	The Laundry List	$9.95
0-932194-40-0	Healing The Child Within	$8.95
0-932194-39-7	Learning To Love Yourself	$7.95
0-932194-25-7	Struggle For Intimacy	$6.95
0-932194-68-0	Twelve Steps To Self-Parenting For Adult Children	$7.95

Orders must be prepaid by check, money order, MasterCard or Visa. Purchase orders from agencies accepted (attach P.O. documentation) for billing. Net 30 days.

TOTAL ORDER VALUE	ADD
$0 - 10.00	$3.00
$10.01 - 25.00	$4.00
$25.01 - 50.00	$4.50
Orders over $50.00 in the U.S.	9%
Orders over $50.00 outside U.S.	15%

* Shipping prices subject to change without prior notice.

Health Communications, Inc.
3201 S.W. 15th Street
Deerfield Beach, FL 33442-8190
(800) 441-5569